National Curriculum History

Medieval Realms
Britain 1066 to 1500

John Simkin

SPROWSTON
WHITE WOMAN LANE
SCHOOL

Spartacus Educational

Contents

1	Primary and Secondary Sources	3
2	The Death of Edward the Confessor	6
3	The Battle of Hastings	7
4	The Norman Conquest	12
5	The Feudal System	14
6	The Medieval Church	17
7	Romanesque and Gothic Architecture	21
8	The Reign of Henry II	24
9	Thomas Becket	27
10	King John and the Magna Carta	30
11	Medieval Art	33
12	The Origins of Parliament	37
13	Edward I in Wales	39
14	The Struggle for Scotland	42
15	The Medieval Village Economy	45
16	Women in the Village Economy	48
17	Alice Sprout of Woolstone	50
18	The Black Death	51
19	The Peasants' Revolt	54
20	Towns and Trade	58
21	The Wars of the Roses	62
	Glossary	65
	Medieval Writers	67

Acknowledgements

Giraudon: front cover, C8:D, C11:A, C11:E, C11:G, C18:B; William Rockwell Nelson: C1:B; V. Prichard: C1:D; Ashmolean Museum: C1:H; Judith Harris: C1:E; C1:G, C3:A, C3:E, C3:F; C6:A, C6:B, C6:C, C6:E, C6:F, C6:H, C7:A, C7:B, C7:C, C7:D, C7:E, C13:F, C13:G, C14:B, C14:D, C17:D, C20:H; Musee de la Tapisserie de Bayeux: C3:D, C3:J; Durham Cathedral: C4:C; Hulton Picture Library: C5:B; Corpus Christi College: C5:B; Scala: C6:K; German National Museum: C7:F; British Library: C9:B, C11:B, C11:C, C11:F, C13:B, C13:D, C15:C, C18:C, C20:J; Bodleian Library: C10:A, C10:B, C10:C; Weidenfeld & Nicolson Archives: C11:D; Osterreichische: C11:H; Bibliotheque Nationale: back cover, C11:J, C19:H; Oxford University: C13:J; Sir David Oglivy: C14:F; Rheinisches Landesmuseum: C16:B, Department of the Environment: C21:A; Mansell Collection: C12:B, C19:A, C19:K; Arrass Library: C21:B.

© Spartacus Educational (1991)
139 Carden Avenue, Brighton, East Sussex, BN1 8NH

All rights reserved. Except for the quotation of short passages for the purposes of criticism and review, no part of this publication may be reproduced, stored in a retrieval system or transmitted in any way or by any means, electronic, mechanical, photocopying, recording or otherwise, without prior permission of Spartacus Educational (Publishers).

1 : Primary and Secondary Sources

This book will be looking at the period 1066 to 1500. When writing about events that took place a long time ago, it is often very difficult to discover exactly what happened. Many sources of information produced at the time have not survived. Those that have include the following written sources:

Annals and Chronicles An annal was a record of what had happened during the year. Many monasteries had a system where monks could note down events that they considered were important. News of these events often came from travellers who stayed at the monastery. Monks who went on trips also brought back information for the annal. Chronicles were like annals but tended to include a more detailed account of events. They were usually the work of one person and therefore tended to be more personal than annals. Chroniclers selected out events they thought were important and tried to explain why they happened.

(B) *The Minstrel*, **an engraving by Durer (1514)**

Eyewitness Accounts Some people wrote books about important events that they saw. For example, in 1170 Edward Grim witnessed the murder of Thomas Becket, the archbishop of Canterbury. A few years later Edward Grim wrote a biography of Thomas Becket which included a detailed description of the murder.

Songs In the Middle Ages minstrels toured the country singing songs in taverns, market-places or any other place where they could find people willing to pay them. These songs often dealt with controversial subjects such as unpopular laws passed by the king and his parliament.

(A) Bridget of Alvastra, woodcut (c. 1498)

(C) A cook and his wife, engraving (c. 1496)

Letters Most letters that have survived from this period were written by government or church officials. However, some families, such as the Pastons from Norfolk, made a copy of all the letters they sent. Although the original letters were usually thrown away, the copies were preserved and can still be read today.

Graffiti Some churches, cathedrals and castles that have survived from this period contain messages that have been scratched on the walls.

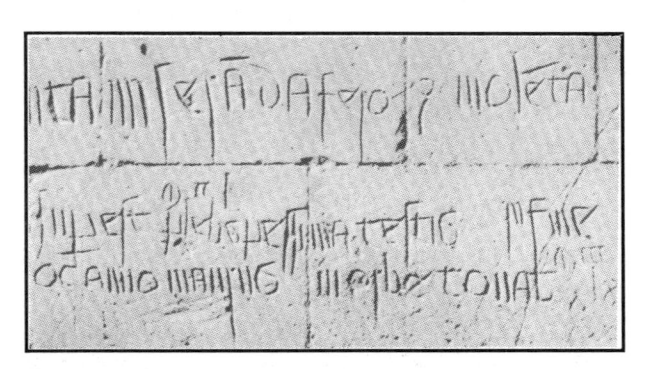

(D) Graffiti found in Ashwell Church in Hertfordshire. The graffiti says "1349: the beginning of the plague. 1350: only the dregs of the population live to tell the tale."

(E) Stained glass window from Tewkesbury Abbey (c. 1345)

Literature Britain produced several extremely talented writers such as Geoffrey Chaucer, William Langland and Marie de France during this period. Poems, plays and novels often provide interesting insights into the way people thought and behaved during the Middle Ages.

Inscriptions Writing can often be found on gravestones, statues and memorials. These inscriptions can sometimes give detailed information on the person that is being remembered.

(F) Woodcut of the devil (1498)

(G) Sculpture above the gateway of St John's College, Cambridge. The sculpture is of Lady Margaret Beaufort, the founder of the college.

Official Records A large collection of official documents have survived from this period. These include government surveys, laws, charters, chirographs, court rolls and pipe rolls.

A large collection of artefacts (objects made by people) have also survived from this period. These include:

Coins and Seals Coins usually showed the face of the monarch that was ruling at the time. One of the great advantages of this for the historian is that coins are normally dated. Kings and other prosperous and powerful people also had their own seals. These seals were used to prove that the document was genuine or to show that it had not been tampered with.

Paintings, Drawings, Engravings, Woodcuts, Tapestries and Sculpture The best information on what people looked like in the medieval period comes from these sources.

(H) A silver groat coin issued by Edward I in 1279.

Buildings These include churches, cathedrals, castles, guild-halls, shops and houses. Some of these have survived intact while others are in ruins.

(I) Beaumaris Castle in Wales. The castle was built between 1295 and 1300.

C1:1 Study sources A-I in this unit and sources B, E and J in chapter 11 (pages 33 to 36). Take one source at a time and explain how each source would help the historian to obtain information about the Middle Ages. (AT3 L5)

C1:2 Look at the section on Medieval writers on pages 67 and 68. Find out what the following two groups of writers have in common: Group A: William of Malmesbury, Matthew Paris, Ordericus Vitalis and Thomas Walsingham; Group B: Marie de France, Margery Kempe, Margaret Paston and Christine de Pisan. Once you have found out what these groups have in common, explain how this might have influenced what they wrote about the Middle Ages. (AT2 L4)

C1:3 Look up the following words in the Glossary (pages 65 and 66): chirographs, charters, court rolls, pipe rolls, testimonials and the Domesday survey. Then explain which of these would be most useful to historians writing books about: (i) town government; (ii) ownership of land in the 11th century; (iii) medieval marriages; (iv) the medieval legal system. (AT3 L5)

C1:4 Imagine you are a historian who wants to write a book about Cecilia of Oxford, an important doctor during the 14th century. What kind of sources would you need to study before you wrote your book? (AT3 L6)

2 : The Death of Edward the Confessor

Edward the Confessor became king of England in 1042. Edward, who had lived in Normandy for 28 years, was not in a strong position and relied heavily on the support of a powerful figure called Godwin of Wessex. To keep Godwin's support, Edward agreed to marry his daughter, Edith. Although he knew he could not become king himself, Godwin hoped that his daughter would be able to produce the next king of England.

This possibility ended when Edward sent Edith to a convent. He also appointed several friends from Normandy to important positions of power in England. Edward now felt strong enough to send Godwin and his sons into exile.

Edward the Confessor, as he became known, seems to have already realised that he was not going to have any children for it is claimed that in 1051 he told William, duke of Normandy, that he wanted him to be the next king of England.

In 1052 the Godwin family returned to England with a large fleet and demanded that Edward's Norman advisers should be sent into exile. Edward's men refused to fight and so the king was forced to accept defeat. It was now Earl Godwin and his sons, rather than the Normans, who helped rule England.

Earl Godwin died in 1053 and his son, Harold, became the head of the family. He led the English army successfully against the Welsh in 1063. Harold's status increased with this victory and he became a strong candidate to become king of England when Edward died.

Harold was an intelligent and easy-going man and Edward eventually grew to like and respect him. In return, Harold remained loyal to Edward.

Edward died on 5 January 1066. The next day there was a meeting of the Witan. The Witan was made up of a group of about sixty lords and bishops who helped govern England. With the death of Edward, the Witan had the responsibility of deciding who should be the next king of England.

A man could become king of Anglo-Saxon England in several different ways: if he was (1) the eldest son or the closest relative of the last king; (2) a man who could show he was descended from previous kings of England; (3) a man designated (chosen) by the previous king; (4) a man who had good leadership qualities; (5) a man who was so powerful that he could take the throne despite the views of the Witan.

There were four main candidates to become king:

Edgar Etheling was Edward the Confessor's great-nephew and his closest relative still alive. Edgar was also a descendant of the Anglo-Saxon's most impressive king, Alfred the Great. Edgar had lived most of his life in Hungary and was only fourteen years old.

Harald Hardrada was king of Norway and claimed that his father Magnus and his descendants had been promised the throne by King Harthacnut (the English king before Edward the Confessor).

Harold of Wessex claimed that Edward the Confessor promised him the throne just before he died.

William of Normandy was the great-nephew of Edward the Confessor's mother. William also claimed that Edward the Confessor promised him the throne in 1051.

C2:1 Look at the five ways you could become king in Anglo-Saxon England. Explain the arguments for and against the four main contenders for the throne and then decide who you think should have become king of England in 1066. (AT1 L4b)

3 : The Battle of Hastings

On 6 January 1066, the Witan decided that Harold was to be the next king of England. The main opposition to Harold came from two brothers, Edwin, earl of Mercia and Morcar, earl of Northumbria. To gain their support Harold married their sister Edith.

King Harold was fully aware that both King Hardrada of Norway and William of Normandy might try to take the throne from him. Harold believed that the Normans posed the main danger and he positioned his troops on the south coast of England.

Harold's soldiers were made up of housecarls and the fyrd. Housecarls were well-trained, full-time soldiers who were paid for their services. The fyrd were working men who were called up to fight for the king in times of danger.

Harold waited all summer but the Normans did not arrive. By September

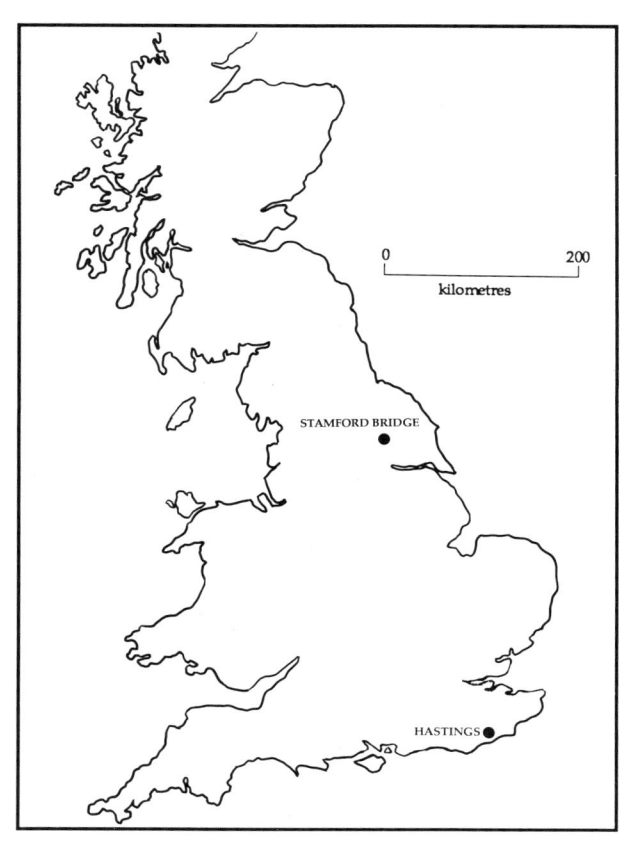

(B) The sites of the battles in 1066.

Harold's army was running out of food. Members of the fyrd were also keen to harvest their own fields and so Harold sent them home. Harold also sent his navy back to London.

William's attack on England had been delayed. To make sure he had enough soldiers to defeat Harold, he asked the men of Poitou, Burgundy, Brittany and Flanders to help. William also arranged for soldiers from Germany, Denmark and Italy to join his army. In exchange for their services, William promised them a share of the land and wealth of England. William also managed to enlist the support of the pope in his campaign to gain the throne of England.

These negotiations took all summer. William also had to arrange the building of the ships to take his large army to England. About 700 ships were ready to sail in August but William had to wait a further month for a change in

(A) Norman knight at a re-enactment of the Battle of Hastings on October 14, 1990.

the direction of the wind.

In early September Harold heard that King Hardrada of Norway had invaded northern England. The messenger told Harold that Hardrada had come to conquer all of England. It is said that Harold replied: "I will give him just six feet of English soil; or, since they say he is a tall man, I will give him seven feet."

With Hardrada was Harold's brother, Tostig, and 300 ships. Harold and what was left of his army headed north. On the way Harold heard that the earls of Mercia and Northumbria had been defeated by Hardrada and were considering changing sides.

Harold's arrival took Hardrada's troops by surprise at a place called Stamford Bridge. It was a hot day and the Norwegians had taken off their byrnies (leather jerkins with sewn-on metal rings). Harold and his English troops devastated the Norwegians and both Hardrada and Tostig were killed. Of the 300 ships that arrived, less than 25 returned to Norway.

While celebrating his victory at a banquet in York, Harold heard that William had landed at Pevensey. Harold immediately assembled the housecarls who had survived the Battle of Stamford Bridge and marched south. Harold travelled at such a pace that many of his troops failed to keep up with him. When Harold arrived in London he waited for the local fyrd to assemble and for the troops of the earls of Mercia and Northumbria to arrive from the north. After five days they had not arrived and so Harold decided to head for the south coast without his northern troops.

When Harold realised he was unable to take William by surprise, he positioned himself at Senlac Hill near Hastings. Harold selected a spot that was protected on each flank by marshy land. At his rear was a forest. The English housecarls provided a shield wall at the front of Harold's army. They carried

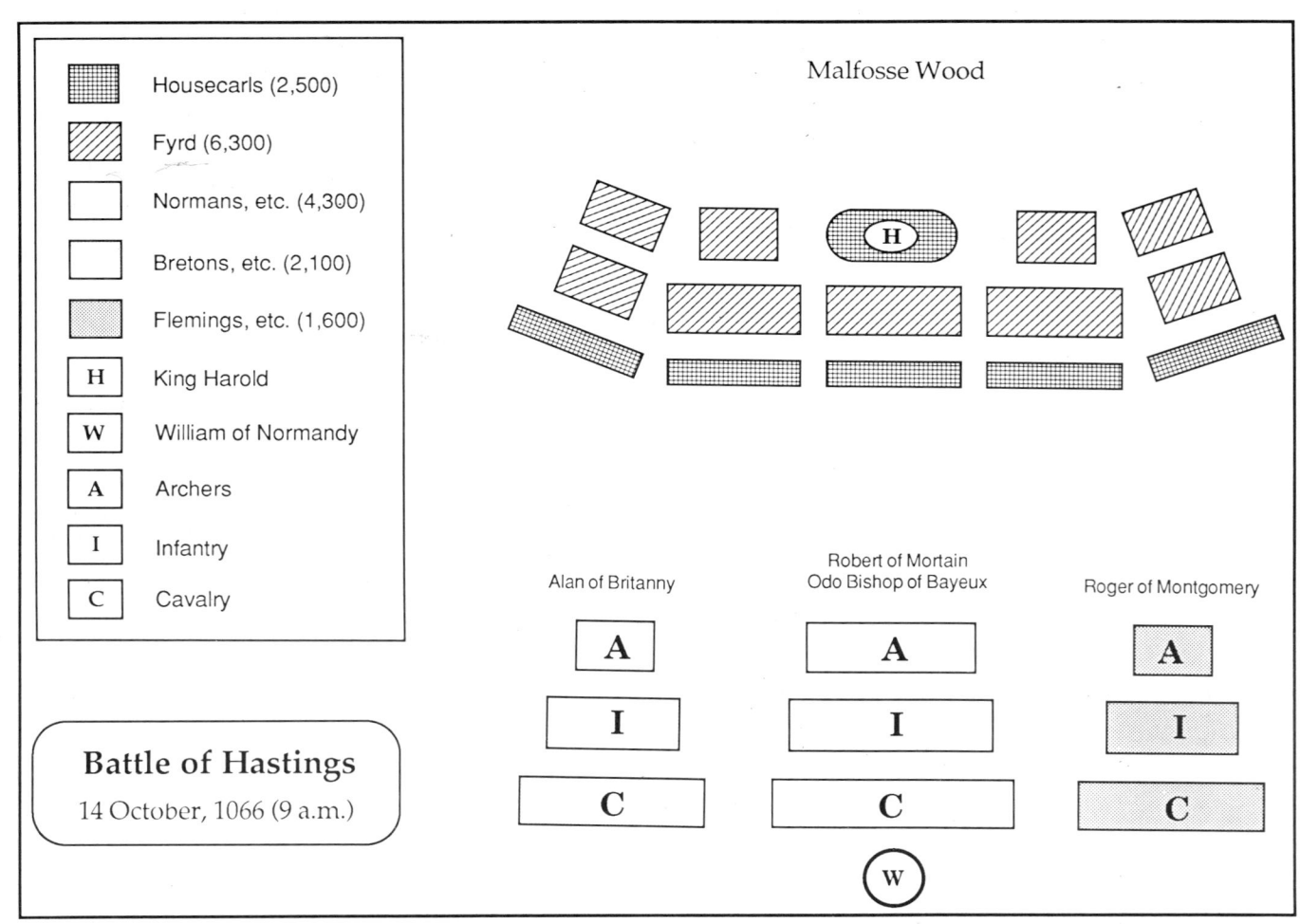

(C) Plan of the Battle of Hastings.

(D) Bayeux Tapestry: "Here English and French fall together in battle" (c. 1090)

large battle-axes and were considered to be the toughest fighters in Europe.

The fyrd were placed behind the housecarls. The leaders of the fyrd, the thanes, had swords and javelins but the rest of the men were inexperienced fighters and carried weapons such as iron-studded clubs, scythes, reaping hooks and hay forks.

We have no accurate figures of the number of soldiers who took part at the Battle of Hastings. Historians have estimated that William had about 5,000 infantry and 3,000 knights while Harold had about 2,000 housecarls and 5,000 members of the fyrd.

Stage 1: At 9.00 a.m. the Norman archers walked up the hill and when they were about a 100 yards away from Harold's army they fired their first batch of arrows. Using their shields, the housecarls were able to block most of this attack. The Norman infantry then charged up the hill.

Stage 2: The English held firm and eventually the Normans were forced to retreat. Members of the fyrd on the right broke ranks and chased after them. A rumour went round that William was amongst the Norman casualties. Afraid of what this story would do to Norman morale, William pushed back his helmet and rode amongst his troops, shouting that he was still alive. He then ordered his cavalry to attack the English who had left their positions on Senlac Hill. English losses were heavy and very few managed to return to the line.

Stage 3: At about 12.00 p.m. there was a break in the fighting for an hour. This gave both sides a chance to remove the

(E) Photograph of English archers taken at a re-enactment of the Battle of Hastings on 14 October 1990.

dead and wounded from the battlefield. William, who had originally planned to use his cavalry when the English retreated, decided to change his tactics. At about one in the afternoon he ordered his archers forward. This time he told them to fire higher in the air. The change of direction of the arrows caught the English by surprise. The arrow attack was immediately followed by a cavalry charge. Casualties on both sides were heavy. Those killed included Harold's two brothers, Gyrth and Leofwin. However, the English line held and the Normans were eventually forced to retreat. The fyrd, this time on the left side, chased the Normans down the hill. William ordered his knights to turn and attack the men who had left the line. Once again the English suffered heavy casualties.

Stage 4: William ordered his troops to take another rest. The Normans had lost a quarter of their cavalry. Many horses had been killed and the ones left alive were exhausted. William decided that the knights should dismount and attack on foot. This time all the Normans went into battle together. The archers fired their arrows and at the same time the knights and infantry charged up the hill.

Stage 5: It was now 4.00 p.m. Heavy English casualties from previous attacks meant that the front line was shorter. The Normans could now attack from the side. The few housecarls that were left were forced to form a small circle round the English standard. The Normans attacked again and this time they broke through the shield wall and Harold and most of his housecarls were killed.

Stage 6: With their king dead, the fyrd saw no reason to stay and fight, and retreated to the woods behind. The Normans chased the fyrd into the woods but suffered further casualties themselves when they were ambushed by the English.

C3:1 Look carefully at source C and stages 1 to 6 of the battle. Draw 6 large boxes or use a copy of the *Battle of Hastings* chart. Choose a different colour or pattern for each group. Now fill in your code box. In each square draw a diagram of what happened at each stage of the battle. Underneath use a couple of sentences to describe the events. (AT1 L4c)

C3:2 Study source H. Select examples from the passage where the author expresses (i) facts, and (ii) opinions. (AT2 L3)

C3:3 There is some doubt about how Harold was killed. Describe how sources H, J, K and L help to answer this question. How reliable is this evidence? Before you answer this question it will help you to read about the authors on pages 67 and 68 and the Bayeux Tapestry on page 65. (AT2 L5)

C3:4 Compare the value of sources F, H and L to the historian writing a book about the Battle of Hastings. (AT3 L6)

(F) Photograph of Norman knights taken at a re-enactment of the Battle of Hastings on 14 October 1990.

(G) Message sent by William just before the battle took place. The message is quoted by William of Poitiers in his book *Deeds of William, Duke of the Normans*. (c. 1071)
With the aid of God I would not hesitate to oppose (the English) ... even if I had only ten thousand... instead of sixty thousand I now command.

(H) Anglo-Saxon Chronicle, Version D (1066)
Then came William duke of Normandy into Pevensey... This was then made known to King Harold, and he then gathered a great force, and came to meet him at the estuary of Appledore; and William came against him unawares before his people were assembled... King Harold was killed... and the French were masters of the field... God granted it to them because of the sins of the people.

(I) Anglo-Saxon Chronicle, Version E (1066)
William landed at Hastings on Michaelmas Day, and Harold came from the north and fought with him before all the army had come, and there he fell and his two brothers Gyrth and Leofwine; and William conquered the country.

(J) Bayeux Tapestry: "Here Harold is killed" (c. 1090)

(K) William of Malmesbury, *Deeds of the Kings of the English* (c. 1140)
The English... passed the night without sleep, in drinking and singing, and, in the morning, proceeded without delay towards the enemy; all were on foot, armed with battle-axes... The king himself on foot, stood, with his brothers, near the standard, in order that, while all shared equal danger, none might think of retreating... On the other side, the Normans passed the whole night in confessing their sins... (The English) few in number and brave in the extreme... fought with ardour, neither giving ground, for great part of the day... Harold fell, his brain pierced by an arrow... One of the soldiers with a sword gashed his thigh as he lay on the ground.

(L) William of Poitiers, *Deeds of William, Duke of the Normans* (c. 1071)
Harold and his two brothers had fallen close together. The king could not be recognised by his face - only by certain marks on his body. His mother offered an equal weight in gold for her son's corpse. But the duke refused, and had the body taken to his own camp.

C3:5 Study sources G, H, I and K. Make a list of the reasons why these writers believed that the English lost the Battle of Hastings. Then explain whether you think these reasons are (a) very important, (b) fairly important, or (c) not very important in explaining Harold's defeat. (AT1 L6b)

4 : The Norman Conquest

The Normans were in poor shape after the Battle of Hastings. However, the English forces lacked a leader. Harold and his brothers were dead and Edgar Etheling was only a teenager.

On his way to London William burnt and looted the villages he passed through. London was well protected and instead of trying to take the capital he went on the rampage in Surrey, Hampshire and Berkshire.

Leading figures in England arranged a meeting with William and offered to accept him as their king if he would stop his campaign of destruction. William agreed and he was crowned king on 25 December, 1066.

William did not keep his promise and Norman soldiers continued to loot and rape without punishment. The land and wealth of England was distributed amongst the knights who had fought on the side of the Normans. In return for the support the pope had given him in his campaign, William dispatched large cargoes of gold to churches in Europe.

The stealing of English property led to fresh conflicts. As the English lacked a national leader, revolts against the Normans were localised. Eadric the Wild, who was active in the Welsh borderlands, and Hereward the Wake in eastern England, were particularly troublesome to the Normans.

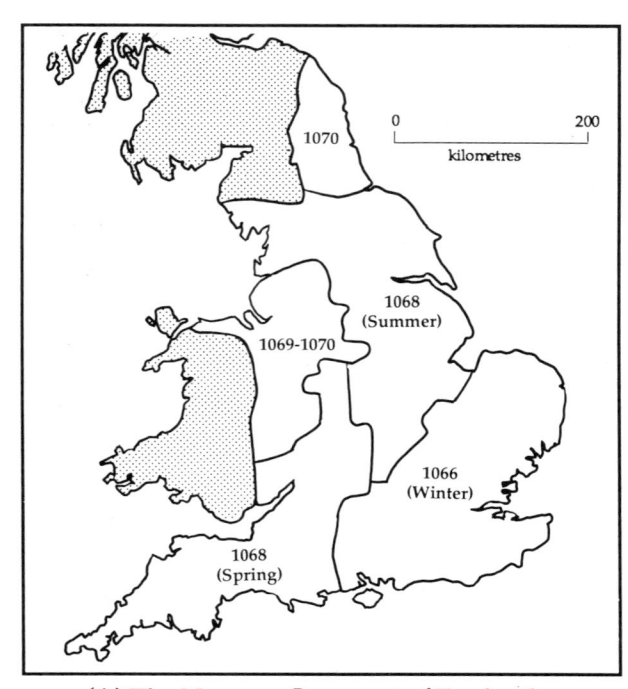

(A) The Norman Conquest of England

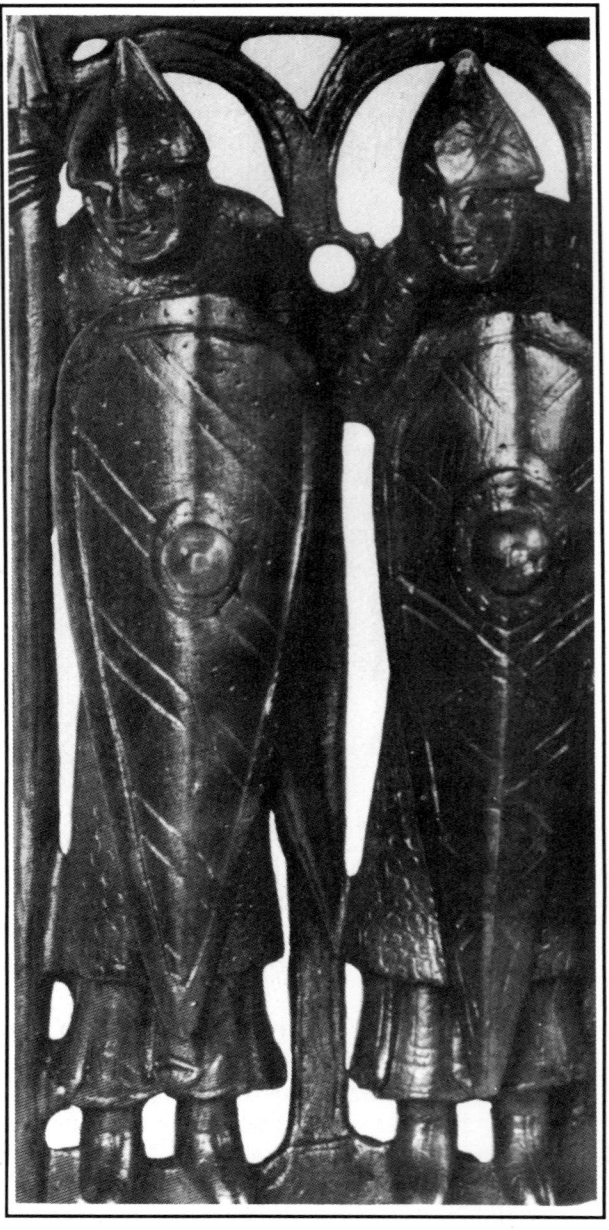

(B) Bronze sculpture of Norman knights (c. 1140)

> **(C) William the Conqueror, quoted by Ordericus Vitalis**
> The Normans... strive to conquer every enemy... They are ready for every sort of crime... They must therefore be restrained by a kind but firm master.

(D) Illustration from a Norman bible (c. 1170)

(G) Norman poem on William the Conqueror (c. 1080)
Your people attacked the region,
Laid it waste, and burnt it with fire...
The foolish folk denied that you were king!
Therefore they perished justly and went to destruction.

The northern areas were in constant revolt and in 1069 the Normans lost control of York. On the march from Durham to York, William the Conqueror ordered that every man or boy that they came across should be killed. Houses, crops, cattle and farming equipment were also destroyed.

This campaign of terror gradually subdued the English people. Twenty years after the Battle of Hastings the old English ruling class had been virtually wiped out. Before the arrival of William there were over 4,000 large landowners. By 1086 only two of these men still held land in England.

(E) William of Malmesbury, *The Deeds of the Kings of the English*, (c. 1140)
After their coming to England they (the Normans) revived the rule of religion which had grown lifeless. They built churches in every village, and, in the towns and cities, monasteries.

C4:1 Take a copy of a map of Britain. Use the information from source A to make a choropleth map. Use different shades of just one colour for each of the following areas: (a) 1066 (Winter); (b) 1068 (Spring); (c) 1068 (Summer); (d) 1069-1070; (e) 1070. Each stage of the Norman Conquest should be done in a slightly darker shade of the colour you have chosen. Explain the advantages of using a choropleth map. (AT1 L3a)

C4:2 Study sources B and D. To what extent do these sources agree on what Norman soldiers looked like? (AT2 L4)

C4:3 The size of William's army was only small compared to the size of the English population. How was William able to take control of England? Source A should help you answer this question. (AT1 L4b)

C4:4 Study source G. How does the author of this source justify the damage caused by the Normans? Do you think Henry of Huntington (source F) would have agreed with the author of source G? (AT2 L4)

C4:5 Select passages from sources E, F and G that illustrate some of the consequences of the Norman invasion. (AT1 L4b) These sources were all written by medieval writers. Does this mean that the information in these sources must be correct? (AT2 L5)

C4:6 What kind of sources would you need to look at if you wanted to discover the impact that the Norman conquest had on England? It will help you to look again at pages 3, 4 and 5 before answering this question. (AT3 L6)

(F) Henry of Huntington, *History of the English* (c. 1130)
The Normans were blinded with greed for gold and silver... William's sheriffs... whose duty was to dispense law and justice, were more savage than the thieves and robbers.

5 : The Feudal System

After his coronation in 1066 William claimed that all the land in England now belonged to him. William retained about a fifth of this land for his own use. The rest was distributed to the those men who had helped him to defeat Harold.

In return for these lands (*fiefs*), the 170 tenants-in-chief had to provide men for military service. The number of knights (horse soldiers) tenants-in-chief had to provide depended on the amount of land they had been given.

In order to supply these knights, tenants-in-chief (also called barons) divided some of their land up into smaller units called manors. These manors were then passed on to men who promised to serve as knights when the king needed them.

William gave a quarter of the land in England to the church. Bishops, abbots and priors that were granted land also had to promise to supply knights. For example, in exchange for his land the archbishop of Canterbury had to provide sixty knights when the king wanted them.

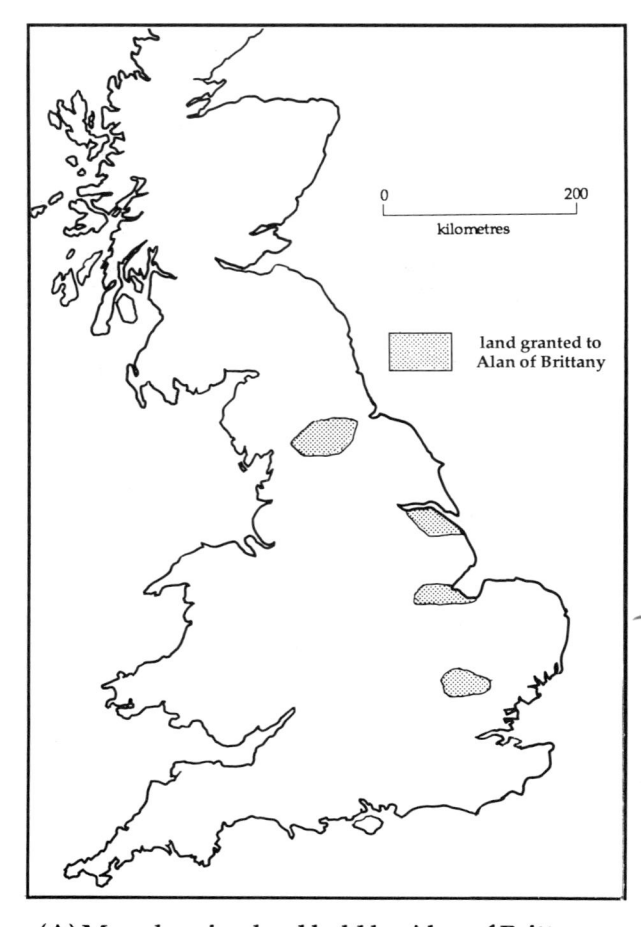

When William granted land to his tenant-in-chief an important ceremony took place. The tenant-in-chief knelt before the king, placed his hands between the king's and said: "I become your man," swearing on the Bible to remain faithful for the rest of his life. The tenant-in-chief would then carry out similar ceremonies with his knights. To break this oath was a very serious crime in Norman England.

By the time William and his tenants-in-chief had finished distributing land, there were about 6,000 manors in England. Manors varied in size, some

(B) Alan of Brittany swears fealty to William in exchange for land in England.

(A) Map showing land held by Alan of Brittany.

having only one village, others including several villages.

The lord of the manor would keep about a third of this land for his own use (the *demesne*). The rest would be divided up between the peasants who lived in the village. Those peasants who were freemen could rent the land for an agreed fee. However, the vast majority of the peasants were unfree. These unfree peasants, who were called villeins or serfs, had to provide a whole range of services in exchange for the land that they used.

The main requirement of the villein was to supply labour service. This involved working on the lord's *demesne* without pay for several days a week. As well as the free labour, the villein also had to provide the oxen plough-team or any equipment that was needed. The lord usually employed a bailiff and a reeve to make sure the work was done to the required standard.

The villein also had to pay his lord a whole range of different taxes and fines. Every year he paid a tax called a *tallage*.

The Reeve was old and choleric and thin;
His beard was shaven closely to his skin...
He could judge by watching drought
                          and rain
The yield he might expect from
                      seed and grain.
His master's sheep, his animals and hens,
Pigs, horses, dairies, stores, and
                      cattle-pens
Were wholly trusted to his government.
He had been under contract to present
The accounts, right from his master's
                      earliest years
No one had ever caught him in arrears.

(C) Geoffrey Chaucer, *Canterbury Tales* (c. 1395)

There was also a toll tax every time he sold an animal. The villein also paid fines when his daughter married (*merchet*) or if she had an illegitimate child (*leyrewite*).

When the head of the villein family died, *heriot* had to be paid to the lord. Heriot enabled the lord to claim the dead villein's best animal. To make matters worse, the local rector had the

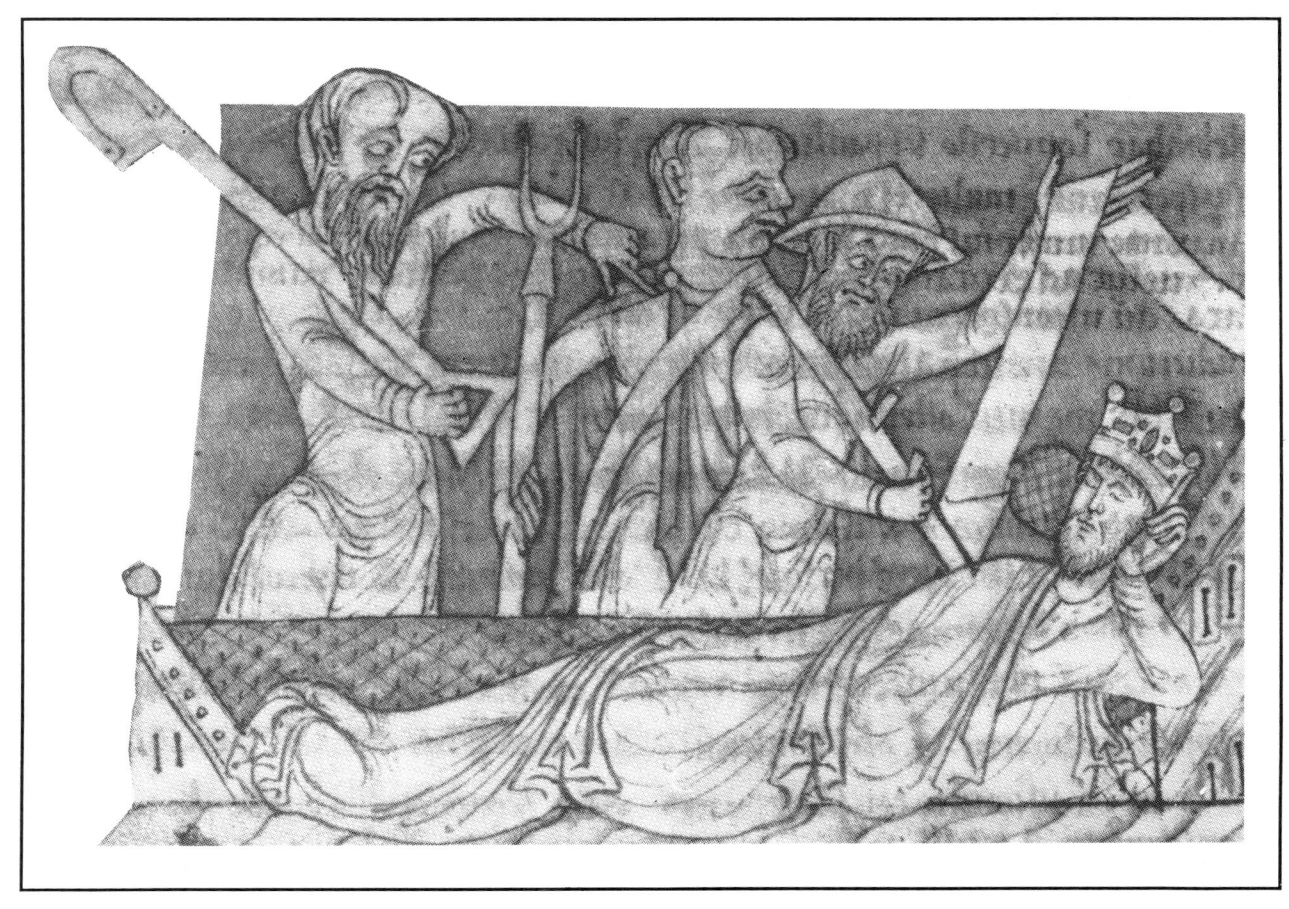

(D) Manuscript painting showing Henry I having a nightmare. (c. 1100)

(E) Message sent by William the Conqueror in 1072.
William, king of the English to Ethelwig, abbot of Evesham, greetings. I order you to... bring with you fully equipped those five knights which you owe me in respect of your abbacy.

(F) Woodcut of a knight. From an early edition of *Canterbury Tales* (c. 1495)

right to take the villein's second-best animal. In order to keep using the lord's land, the family also had to pay an entry fee.

The villein had no say in the rules that a lord might impose. For example, the villein might be forced to use his lord's mill or oven at inflated prices. However, the thing that usually upset the villeins most was that they were considered to be the property of the lord. This meant that they could not leave the lord's manor without his permission.

The system of being granted land in exchange for military or labour service was called feudalism. The Normans found feudalism to be a good way of controlling people and the system was used in all the lands they conquered.

C5:1 Study sources A and B. Explain why Alan of Brittany's land came in four plots rather than one larger plot. You will find source A on page 12 will help you with this answer. (AT1 L3b)

C5:2 Study source D. Why do you think the artist described the painting as the king's nightmare? (AT3 L3)

C5:3 Explain how Ethelwig of Evesham (source E) would have been able to provide five fully equipped knights for William the Conqueror. (AT1 L4c)

C5:4 William the Conqueror's introduction of the feudal system brought great change to land ownership in England. Explain whether these changes were rapid or gradual and whether they were local or national. (AT1 L5a) Do you think the people living in England at the time approved of these changes? Explain your answer in as much detail as possible. (AT1 L6a)

C5:5 What type of sources would a historian need to look at when writing a book about the feudal system? (AT3 L6)

C5:6 Study source C and read about Chaucer on page 67. What are the strengths and weaknesses of this source to a historian writing about feudalism in the Middle Ages? (AT2 L7)

(G) Villein services in the village of Holkham (c. 1260)
Roger Haven and Harvey Carpenter hold 32 acres for 26d... and will carry half a measure of dung... and 16 works in Autumn and 3 boon-works in Autumn... and will thrash for 32 days... and 2 boon-works with a plough... and will weed for 3 half days... and will go to the pond 4 times and pay 4 hens.

6 : The Medieval Church

Most lords of the manor arranged for a church to be built in the villages they controlled. The lord also appointed a rector to look after religious matters in the manor. With the job went a house and some land known as the glebe.

The rector also received a tax, called a tithe, from the villagers. This was usually a tenth of the crops that had been produced during the year. With this money the rector had to pay for church repairs and to help people in need.

If the rector had a large parish under his control, there would probably be several churches to look after. The rector would therefore appoint a priest, called a vicar, to look after each one of these churches. These men were often the sons of peasants and had received very little education. Rectors usually paid these priests very small wages. As rectors were often fairly wealthy people, village priests sometimes felt they were being unfairly treated. This helps to explain why several priests took part in the Peasants' Revolt in 1381.

Church services were held every day but most people in the village did not go to them during the week. However, everybody in the village was expected to attend Mass on Sunday mornings. If people constantly failed to attend Mass, they were likely to end up in the church court.

As the church service was held in Latin, the vast majority of people who attended the service did not understand what was being said. This was also true of some of the priests who had only been taught to memorise the text of the service. Not surprisingly, visiting bishops often complained that villagers were guilty of talking and laughing

(A) Greensted Church was originally built in the 9th century. It is the only surviving Anglo-Saxon wooden church in Britain. The chancel on the right was added by the Normans and then rebuilt in the 16th century. The tower on the left was added in the 17th century.

during church services.

The church service would also usually include a sermon. This was given in English and had more chance of holding people's attention. These sermons usually involved stories from the Bible or dealt with the subject of sin. Christians were constantly being warned of the danger of going to hell when they died. This message was reinforced by paintings on the walls of the church that showed terrifying scenes of sinners being tortured in hell.

As well as going to Sunday Mass, villagers also attended the parish church for marriages and funeral services. People also had their children baptised in church. They did this as soon as the children were born, as they believed that if you were unbaptised you would go to hell when you died. Villagers were also expected to visit the church to confess their sins to the priest and be told what penance they had to perform.

Each parish was part of a larger area called a diocese. A bishop, based in a large town with a cathedral, was in overall control of the diocese. The bishop or his assistant, an archdeacon, were supposed to make regular visits to the churches in their diocese to make sure the priests were doing their job properly.

Some religious people, called monks and nuns, decided to withdraw themselves from the world so they could dedicate themselves to God. Most of the monks in England followed the rules first proposed by St Benedict of

(C) Westham Church. It is claimed that this was the first church built by the Normans after they conquered England in 1066.

(B) Anglo-Saxon church in Sompting that was built in the 11th century. The style is known as 'Rhenish Helm' or 'Rhineland Helmet'.

To save and to spare and to spend upon
 the needy,
As Christ himself commands of all
 Christian people...
Thus patient poverty is the most
 perfect living,
And all priests who seek perfection
 should draw towards poverty.

(D) William Langland, *Piers Plowman* (c. 1365)

(E) St. John's Church, Great Maplestead. The church was built in about 1340 by a group of knights who had taken part in the Crusades. It is one of only four round medieval churches in Britain.

Nursia in 529. When they first entered the monastery Benedictine monks made three promises, known as vows. These vows concerned poverty (they were not allowed to own things), chastity (they were not allowed to marry) and obedience (they had to obey their abbot who ran the monastery).

Many monasteries were given land by William the Conqueror when he took over England in 1066. Rich people also left land and money to monasteries when they died because they thought it would help them go to heaven. Over a period of time many monasteries became very wealthy. Some used this wealth to help the poor, but others kept it to make life easier for themselves. For example, the records of one monastery in Durham reveal that the monks employed butlers, valets, pages, grooms, gardeners, washer-women and jesters.

Some people were very critical of the way that Benedictine monks were behaving, and other religious orders were formed. One of the most important of these was the Cistercian Order. First founded in 1098, the Cistercians were determined to keep strictly to the rules first laid down by St Benedict. They held church services eight times a day and when they were not praying they worked hard in the fields. The Cistercians avoided all luxuries and even though they were successful farmers they kept to a simple vegetarian diet. So that they would not be tempted by the way other people lived, the Cistercians tended to site their monasteries in remote areas.

Others who were critical of the way that monks were living joined the Franciscans. The Franciscan Order had originally been founded by Francis of Assisi, the son of a wealthy Italian merchant, who gave up his life of luxury to help the poor. The first Franciscan friars arrived in England in 1224. Unlike the monks, the Franciscan friars lived amongst the people. The friars pointed out that Jesus was not only poor himself but spent his life helping the poor. Franciscans tried to follow the example set by Jesus and did a great deal to help those suffering from poverty.

(F) Painting of St. Christopher on the wall of Pickering Church. It was believed in the Middle Ages that if you looked at a picture of St. Christopher every day you would not die.

(G) Extract from the will left by Margaret Paston. (1484)
Ten marks for an honest priest to sing and pray in Mautby Church for my soul, the souls of my father and mother, the soul of my late husband John Paston, and for the souls of his ancestors and mine, during the seven years after my death.

(H) Medieval wall-paintings in the chancel of Copford Church. The stained glass window was added in the 19th century.

(I) Records from the Syon Monastery in Sheen, near London (c. 1140)
Whoever comes to the monastery, on any day of the year, and gives something for the repair of the monastery... shall have five hundred days of pardon.

(J) Report sent to the Bishop of Norwich describing a sermon given by the Lollard, Margery Baxter. (1427)
Margery Baxter... cursed... cardinals, archbishops... and especially the bishop of Norwich... for their laws to take money from the poor folk.

C6:1 Study sources F and H. Explain why pictures were painted on the walls of churches during the Middle Ages. (AT1 L3b)

C6:2 Give as many reasons as you can why the Church became very wealthy during the Middle Ages. Include information from sources G and I in your answer. (AT1 L4c)

C6:3 Many monasteries became very wealthy during the Middle Ages. Did this process happen rapidly or gradually? (AT1 L5a)

C6:4 Why were some people unhappy about the growing wealth of the Church? What action did they take? Refer to sources D, J and K in your answer. (AT1 L5c)

C6:5 Study sources A, B, C and E. What evidence is there in these sources that the design of churches changed between the 9th and 14th centuries? (AT1 L3c) Give as many reasons as you can why there were changes in church design during this period. (AT1 L6c)

(K) Medieval painting showing Franciscan nuns. These nuns became known as "Poor Clares".

7 : Romanesque and Gothic Architecture

William the Conqueror was unimpressed by Anglo-Saxon buildings when he arrived in England in 1066. He ordered that cathedrals and abbeys should be pulled down and replaced by those built in the Norman style. To impress the English, William constructed buildings that were even larger than those in Normandy.

The Normans recruited master-masons from all over Europe to design and build their cathedrals, abbeys and castles. Many of these master masons came from southern Italy and Sicily, an area conquered by the Normans in 1042.

The main problem facing master-masons designing large buildings was to find a way of preventing the roof from collapsing. At first the Normans solved this problem by copying methods developed by the Romans. They had discovered that by cutting blocks of stone that were slightly wedge-shaped, it was possible to build a semi-circular arch. The centre of the arch did not collapse because the pressure from the side walls held the centre in place. By constructing a series of these arches it was possible to roof a whole building

(A) One of Durham Cathedral's windows.

(B) Durham Cathedral

(C) Lincoln Cathedral's chapter-house.

using this technique. This type of roof was called a barrel vault because it looked like a barrel cut down the middle.

The Normans, like the Romans, experimented with a whole range of different types of vaulted roofs. For example, the groin vault was formed by the intersection at right angles of two barrel vaults.

The buildings constructed by the Normans in the 11th century were not unlike those built by the Romans and this is why they are often referred to as being in the Romanesque style.

In the 12th century there was a demand for large stained-glass windows in churches and cathedrals. As these large windows weakened the structure of the building, extra supports, called buttresses, were added to the outside walls. Sometimes these supports took the form of a half-arch and were known as flying buttresses.

In the middle of the 12th century masons began to introduce the pointed arch. It also become popular to add extra ribs to the groin vault. Later, these new buildings with their pointed arches, flying buttresses and ribbed vaults were decribed as being built in the Gothic style.

(D) Salisbury Cathedral.

(E) Exeter Cathedral's ribbed (fan) vault.

C7:1 Look at sources A, C, D and E. Are these examples of Romanesque or Gothic buildings? (AT1 L3c)

C7:2 Study source F in this unit and source H on page 35. Explain the different jobs the men are doing. (AT3 L3)

C7:3 Look up 'manuscript paintings' and 'woodcuts' on page 66. Then explain which of these two visual sources would be most useful to a historians studying architecture in the 12th century. (AT3 L5)

C7:4 Durham Cathedral (source B) was built close to the Scottish border. It has been described as being a work of 'Norman propaganda'. Look up the word propaganda on the sheet *Source Material Key Words* and then explain what the writer meant by this. (AT1 L7c)

(F) A manuscript drawing (c. 1460)

23

8 : The Reign of Henry II

Henry I, the son of William the Conqueror, became king of England in 1100. Although he married twice, Henry only had two legitimate children, William and Matilda. (He had at least another twenty outside marriage.) When his son William drowned in 1120, Henry decided to ask his barons to accept his daughter as the country's next ruler. The barons were not happy about this but after much discussion they accepted Henry's request.

When Henry I died in 1135, some of the barons did not keep their promise to support Matilda. The Normans had never had a woman leader. Norman law stated that all property and rights should be handed over to men. To the Normans this meant that her husband Geoffrey of Anjou, would become their next ruler.

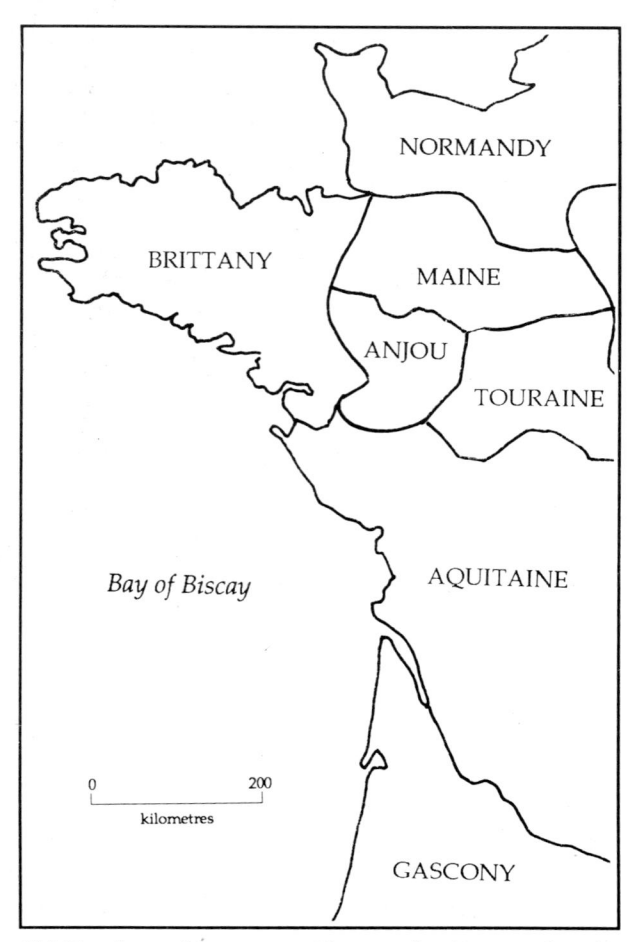

(B) Painting of Matilda (c. 1875)

The people of Anjou (Angevins) were considered to be barbarians by the Normans. Most Normans were unwilling to accept an Angevin ruler and instead decided to help Stephen, the son of one of William the Conqueror's daughters, to become king.

For the next eighteen years there was civil war between the supporters of Matilda and Stephen. As neither side was strong enough to achieve an outright victory, the result was a long conflict that created a great deal of hardship for the people of England.

Matilda and Geoffrey of Anjou had three sons. At the age of fourteen Henry, the eldest son, arrived in England from Anjou with his own army to help his mother in her fight against Stephen. Young Henry also fought in France, and with his father managed to capture Normandy from Stephen. Later, when Geoffrey died, Henry became the new leader of the Angevins.

It was now clear to the barons that Stephen would never be able to achieve total victory over Matilda. They put pressure on Stephen to bring an end to

(A) Territory in western Europe in 1180 under the control of Henry II.

the civil war and in 1153 negotiations began between the two sides. It was eventually agreed by the Treaty of Westminster that Stephen would remain king until he died. In return, Stephen had to accept Matilda's son Henry as his heir.

Henry did not have to wait long to become king as Stephen died the following year. Henry was now the undisputed ruler of the empire that had been created by his great grandfather, William the Conqueror.

From an early age Henry had been trained as the next king of England. Queen Matilda had employed the best scholars in Europe to educate her son. Henry was a willing student and never lost his love of learning.

When he became king Henry arranged for the world's best scholars to visit his court so that he could discuss important issues with them. One of his close friends said that Henry had a tremendous memory and rarely forgot anything he was told.

(D) Sculpture of Eleanor of Aquitaine and her first husband, Louis VII of France. Henry II acquired Aquitaine, the richest province in France, when he married Eleanor in 1152. (c. 1195)

Henry spent many hours studying Roman history. He was particularly interested in the way Emperor Augustus had successfully managed to gain control over the Roman Empire. Henry realised that, like Augustus, his first task must be to tackle those that had the power to remove him.

This meant that Henry had to control England's powerful barons. His first step was to destroy all the castles that had been built during Stephen's reign. Henry also announced that, in future, castles could only be built with his permission. The new king also deported all the barons' foreign mercenaries.

Henry then took action to unite the people of England. He allowed several of Stephen's officials to keep their government posts. Another strategy used by Henry was to arrange marriages between rival families.

(C) Drawing of Geoffrey of Anjou and his grandson, William Longespee. (c 1151)

Once Henry had complete control over England, he turned his attention to the rest of the British Isles. In 1157 he forced the king of Scotland, Malcolm IV, to surrender Northumberland, Cumberland and Westmorland to England. Henry also invaded Wales and Ireland, but their successful use of guerrilla tactics made complete control over these countries impossible.

A great deal of Henry's reign was spent at war with rivals who wanted to take over the territory he controlled in Europe. Not only did Henry manage to successfully protect this territory, but was able to add to his empire making him the most powerful monarch in Western Europe.

When Henry was in England he spent most of the time travelling. Henry believed that it was important that people saw their ruler as much as possible. He argued that this encouraged the people to remain loyal to their king.

King Henry was full of energy. When he was not working on government business he loved hunting. Even when he arrived back home it was said he rarely sat down.

Henry, unlike most kings, cared little for appearances. He preferred hard-wearing hunting clothes to royal robes. Henry also disliked the pomp and ceremony that went with being king.

Henry believed people had to earn respect. He was often rude to members of the nobility. He was quick to lose his temper and often upset important people by shouting at them. Yet, when dealing with the poor or a defeated enemy, Henry had a reputation for being polite and kind. He also had a great sense of humour and even enjoyed a joke at his own expense.

C8:1 Study source C. What do you notice about the two men's shields? Why did painting pictures on shields become popular during the Middle Ages? (AT1 L3b)

C8:2 Henry II spent twenty-one of the thirty-four years of his reign on the continent. Select information from the sources in this unit to explain why Henry II spent so little time in England. (AT3 L4)

C8:3 Put the following events in the order that they took place and explain the connection between them: (a) The Treaty of Westminster; (b) The death of Henry I; (c) The civil war between Stephen and Matilda; (d) The death of Henry I's son William. (AT1 L5c)

C8:4 Compare the value of sources B, D, E and F to a historian writing a book about the reign of Henry II. (AT3 L6)

C8:5 Give as many reasons as you can why the English people were willing to accept Henry as their king. Explain the different motives people had for supporting him. Use information from the text and the sources in your answer. (AT1 L7c)

(E) William of Newburgh, *History of English Affairs* (c. 1200)
After the miseries they had endured the people hoped for better things from the new monarch, especially as Henry gave signs... of a strict regard for justice... In the early days he gave serious attention to public order and exerted himself to revive the laws of England, which seemed under King Stephen to be dead and buried.

(F) Gerald of Wales, *The Conquest of Ireland* (c. 1190)
No one can doubt how splendidly, how vigorously, how skillfully our most excellent king has practised armed warfare against his enemies in time of war... He not only brought strong peace in England... he won victories in remote and foreign lands.

(G) *The Chronicles of Peter of Blois* (c. 1185)
With King Henry II it is school every day, constant conversation with the best scholars and discussions of intellectual problems... He does not linger in his palaces like other kings but hunts through the country inquiring into what everyone was doing, especially judges whom he has made judges of others.

9 : Thomas Becket

Thomas Becket was the son of a successful London merchant. After being educated in England, France and Italy, he joined the staff of Theobald, the archbishop of Canterbury.

When Henry II became king he asked Archbishop Theobald, the most important religious leader in England, for advice on choosing his government ministers. On the suggestion of Theobald, Henry appointed Thomas Becket as his chancellor.

(A) Drawing from the book *Life of St. Thomas*. The picture shows Becket (left) denouncing the Constitution of Clarendon. (c. 1210)

Thomas Becket's job was an important one. It involved him working very closely with the king, and the two men soon became very close friends. Becket carried out many tasks for Henry II including leading the English army into battle in France.

When Theobald died, Henry chose Thomas Becket as his next archbishop of Canterbury. This decision angered many leading churchmen. They pointed out that Becket had never been a priest, had a reputation as a cruel military commander and was very materialistic (Becket loved expensive food, wine and clothes). They also feared that as Becket was a close friend of Henry II he would not be an independent leader of the church.

Thomas Becket was upset by these criticisms and was determined to be a good archbishop. For the first time Becket began to show a concern for the poor. Every morning thirteen poor people were brought to his home. After washing their feet Becket served them a meal. He also gave each one of them four silver pennies.

Instead of wearing expensive clothes Becket now wore a simple monastic habit. As a penance (punishment for previous sins) he slept on a cold stone floor, wore a tight-fitting hairshirt that was covered in fleas and was scourged (whipped) daily by his monks.

In 1163 Henry arrived back in England after a long spell in France. Henry was told that while he had been away there had been a dramatic increase in serious crime. His officials claimed

(B) *The Martyrdom of St Thomas Becket*. A picture that appeared in a book produced by Ramsey Abbey. (c. 1300)

that since the beginning of his reign they had arrested over a hundred people for murder, but they could not punish them because they had the right to be tried in church courts.

It was not only the clergy who were tried in church courts. Many men who had been trained by the church did not join the clergy. For example, some men who had been taught to read and write became clerks instead. Because they had been trained by the church these men could choose to be tried in church courts for crimes they had committed. This was to their advantage, as church courts could not impose punishments that involved violence such as execution or mutilation. There were several examples of clergy found guilty of murder or robbery who only received "spiritual" punishments such as suspension from office or banishment from the altar.

Henry decided that clergy found guilty of serious crimes should be handed over to his courts. At first Becket agreed with Henry on this issue. After a meeting with church leaders in January 1164, Henry published the Clarendon Constitution. This limited church authority in England and gave the king the right to punish clerics found guilty in church courts.

Some churchmen blamed Becket for the Clarendon Constitution and claimed he was under the control of Henry II. This criticism hurt Becket and was probably partly responsible for him changing his mind on the subject.

Henry was furious when Becket began to argue that the church must retain control of punishing its own clergy. The king believed that Becket was guilty of betrayal and was determined to obtain revenge.

In 1164 the archbishop of Canterbury was involved in a dispute over land. Henry ordered Becket to appear before his courts. When he refused, the king confiscated his property.

Henry now claimed that Becket had stolen £300 of the government's money when he had been chancellor. Becket denied the charge but, so that the matter could be settled, he offered to repay the money. Henry refused this offer and insisted that Becket had to stand trial.

(D) A woodcut published in about 1490. The picture shows a saint (possibly Thomas Becket) performing a miracle.

(C) Stone carving of Thomas Becket in the nave of Exeter Cathedral. (c. 1350)

(E) A woodcut of Thomas Becket that appeared in a book in 1512.

When Henry talked about other charges, including treason, Becket decided to run away to France.

Under the protection of Henry's old enemy, King Louis VII, Becket organised a propaganda campaign against Henry. As Becket was supported by the pope, Henry feared that he would be excommunicated.

Becket eventually agreed to return to England. However, as soon as he arrived he excommunicated the archbishop of York and other leading churchmen who had supported Henry while he had been away. Henry, who was in Normandy at the time, was very angry when he heard the news and was reported to have said: "Will no one rid me of this turbulent priest?"

Four of Henry's knights who heard this outburst decided to travel to England to visit Becket. When they arrived at Canterbury Cathedral in December 1170, the four knights demanded that Becket pardon the churchmen he had excommunicated. When he refused, they killed him.

The Christian world was shocked by Becket's murder. The pope canonised Becket and he became a symbol of Christian resistance to the power of the monarchy. His shrine at Canterbury became the most important place in the country for pilgrims to visit.

Although Henry admitted that his comments had led to the death of Becket, he argued that he had neither commanded nor wished the man's death. In 1172 Pope Alexander III accepted these arguments and absolved Henry from Thomas Becket's murder. In return, Henry had to provide 200 men for a crusade to the Holy Land and had to agree to being whipped by eighty monks. Most importantly of all, Henry agreed to drop his plans to have criminal clerics tried in his courts.

C9:1 Give as many reasons as you can why Henry II appointed Thomas Becket as (a) chancellor; (b) archbishop of Canterbury. (AT1 L5c)

C9:2 How did Becket's behaviour change after he was appointed archbishop of Canterbury? Give some possible reasons for these changes. (AT1 L4c)

C9:3 Why did Henry issue the Clarendon Constitution in 1164? Give as many reasons as you can for Henry's decision. (AT1 L6c)

C9:4 Describe what is taking place in sources A, B, C, D, E and F. Select those sources that provide information on the death of Thomas Becket. (AT3 L5) Do these sources agree about the way Becket died? If so, does this mean that Becket died in this way? (AT2 L5)

(F) Henry II at Canterbury Cathedral in 1172.

10 : King John and the Magna Carta

John was the youngest of Henry II's eight children. He was said to be Henry's favourite, and when he reached the age of seventeen, the king attempted to find territory for him to rule. At first he was given Aquitaine in France but Richard the Lionheart, who was heir to the throne, objected, and in 1184 there was an armed clash between the two brothers.

After Richard's victory Henry decided to give Ireland to John to rule. John proved unpopular with the Irish people and within six months he was forced to come back to England.

These two failures at obtaining territory resulted in him acquiring the nickname 'Lackland'. John was desperate to govern his own land. Aware that his ageing father could do

(A) 'Irish Navigation' from Gerald of Wales' *The Topography of Ireland*. Gerald of Wales had accompanied John to Ireland in 1185.

little to help him, John decided to change sides. In 1189 John joined with his brother, Richard and Philip Augustus, the king of France in an attempt to overthrow his father.

Henry was forced to accept a humiliating peace treaty and soon afterwards died. He had been devastated by the news of John's betrayal and was said to have died of a broken heart.

Richard the Lionheart, who was the new king of England, gave John vast estates as a reward for his help.

(B) 'An Irish Feud' from Gerald of Wales' *The Topography of Ireland*.

However, when Richard went off on his crusades, it was his mother Eleanor, rather than his brother John, who he left in charge of his empire.

For the next ten years John constantly plotted to overthrow his brother. He was no match for Richard or Eleanor and these attempts ended in failure.

Although Richard was married for eight years he did not father any children. When he died in 1199 John became king. Some of the barons in the French part of his empire wanted Arthur of Brittany, the son of John's

(C) 'An Irish Feast' from Gerald of Wales' *Topography of Ireland*. The picture shows Irish men eating horse meat.

dead brother Geoffrey, to be king. Once again John had to fight to assert his authority. This time he was more successful and Arthur was captured and imprisoned. Arthur was never seen again and many people believed that John had arranged for his young rival to be murdered.

Even without their leader, the rebellious barons in France refused to surrender and John became involved in a long-drawn-out war. This was an expensive business and John was forced to introduce new taxes to pay for the war. This created a great deal of resentment in England, and John's standing was not helped when in 1205 his army lost control of Normandy, Brittany, Anjou and Maine. John now had a new nickname; 'Soft-sword'.

John's problems became even more serious after 1205 when he became involved in an argument with the pope over who should become the new archbishop of Canterbury. John favoured his secretary, John de Gray, whereas Pope Innocent III wanted Stephen Langton. Although Langton was an Englishman he had lived in Rome for several years and had never met King John. When John refused to accept the pope's nomination he was excommunicated. The pope also laid an Interdict on England. This meant that except for baptisms and confessions made by the dying, all church services had to be suspended.

John realised that he could not survive against the combined opposition of his barons and the church and decided to do a deal with the pope. The terms of the agreement were harsh. Not only was John forced to accept Stephen

(D) 19th century engraving of Richard the Lionheart.

as archbishop of Canterbury, he also had to agree to the pope becoming his overlord. John was now the pope's vassal and England was a fief of the papacy.

This humiliation only added to the barons' dissatisfaction with King John. His policy of high taxation continued and this was made worse by growing inflation.

In 1215 John made another attempt at gaining control of his lost territory in France. Once again he was defeated and was forced to pay 60,000 marks for a five-year truce. When John tried to obtain this money by imposing another tax, the barons rebelled. Some barons remained loyal but in most areas, especially in the

> (E) Roger of Wendover, *Flowers of History* (c. 1235)
> King John, when he saw that he was deserted by almost all... he deceitfully pretended to make peace for a time with the barons, and sent messengers to them, and told them that, for the sake of peace... he would willingly grant them the laws and liberties they required... At length, after much thought... he devised plans to gain revenge on the barons... He sent Pandulph the Pope's subdeacon to the court of Rome... He also sent messengers to the continent to obtain supplies of troops in those parts, promising them lands... and no small sum of money.

(F) Selected extracts from the Magna Carta (1215)

(I) In the first place we have granted to God... that the English Church shall be free... freedom of elections, which is reckoned most important and very essential to the English Church...

(VIII) No widow shall be compelled to marry, so long as she prefers to live without a husband...

(XII) No scutage or aid (tax) shall be imposed on our kingdom, unless by common counsel of our kingdom...

(XIV) And for obtaining the common counsel of the kingdom before the assessing of an aid or of a scutage, we will cause to be summoned the archbishops, bishops, abbots, earls, and greater barons...

(XXIII) No village or individual shall be compelled to make bridges or river banks...

(XXXIX) No freeman shall be taken or imprisoned or outlawed or exiled or in anyway destroyed... except by the lawful judgement of his peers or by the law of the land...

(XLV) We will appoint as justices, constables, sheriffs, or bailiffs only such as know the law of the kingdom and mean to observe it well...

(XXXV) Let there be one measure of wine throughout the whole kingdom, and one measure of ale; and one measure of corn; and one width of cloth...

north, John had very little support. John had no chance of success and on 15 June 1215, at Runnymede in Surrey, he was forced to accept the peace terms of those who fought against him. This involved John signing the Magna Carta. In this charter John made a long list of promises, including no new taxes without the support of his barons, a reduction in the power of his sheriffs and the right of a fair trial to all freemen.

As soon as John had signed the charter he appealed to the pope for help. As the pope was King John's overlord, he had good reason to be concerned about this rebellion. His response was to excommunicate the barons and to announce that this "vile and base" charter was annulled. In return, John promised to join a new crusade to Jerusalem that the pope was organising.

The pope's ruling led to the resumption of the civil war. Before the conflict could be resolved, John died. During the next ten years the Magna Carta was reissued three times. However, monarchs continued to ignore the terms of the charter.

C10:1 Why did King John have two nicknames? (AT1 L3a)

C10:2 Explain why sources A, B and C give a negative picture of the Irish people. Why might Henry II and John have encouraged Gerald of Wales to produce a book that was critical of the Irish? (AT2 L6)

C10:3 Study source E. Select examples from the passage where the author expresses (a) facts, and (b) opinions. (AT2 L3)

C10:4 Give as many reasons as you can why the barons rebelled against King John in 1215. Divide these into 'short-term' and 'long-term' reasons why they rebelled. (AT1 L5b)

C10:5 Explain why the pope excommunicated the barons and annulled the Magna Carta. Select passages from the sources to support your answer. (AT3 L4)

C10:6 What are the strengths and weaknesses of sources C, D and F to a historian writing about the reign of King John? (AT3 L5)

11 : Medieval Art

(A) Painting from Duke of Berry's *Book of Hours* (c. 1410)

(B) Christine de Pisan presenting one of her books to Isabel of Bavaria. The picture was painted by Christine's friend, Anastasia, in about 1410.

(C) Manuscript painting of textile workers (c. 1400)

(D) Manuscript painting entitled *Autumn* (c. 1500)

(E) Painting from Berry's *Book of Hours* (c. 1410)

(F) Painting from the *Luttrell Psalter* (c. 1325)

(G) Painting from Duke of Berry's *Book of Hours* (c. 1410)

(H) Manuscript painting showing the building of a church (1448)

(I) *Children's Games* by Peter Bruegel (1560)

(J) Manuscript painting of the Battle of Crecy (c. 1460)

12 : The Origins of Parliament

Kings in the Middle Ages would often consult their tenants-in-chief before making important decisions. These men were usually called to appear before the king during religious festivals (Christmas, Easter, Whitsun). Some of the men who attended these meetings were given specific jobs to perform for the king, for example to act as treasurer.

Some kings tended to ignore the advice of their barons. When this led to bad decisions the barons became angry. This is one of the reasons why the barons rebelled against King John and made him sign the Magna Carta.

Henry III was another king who tended to ignore the advice of his barons. Under the leadership of Simon de Montfort, the barons rebelled. They not only demanded the right to have regular meetings with the king, but also insisted they should have a say in the

(A) *A Song Against King Edward II's Taxes* (c. 1320)
A king ought not to go out of his kingdom to make war, unless the commons of his land consent... (the taxes needed for the war) forces the common people to sell cows and clothes... Since the king is determined to make war so much... he should take the money from the rich.

appointment of the king's senior officials. In 1258 Henry III agreed to these demands when he signed the Provisions of Oxford.

After the Battle of Lewes in 1264, Simon de Montfort took control of the council which had now become known as parliament (*parler* was Norman French for talk). The following year Simon de Montfort expanded parliament by inviting representatives from the shires and towns to attend the meetings. However, later that year, Simon de Montfort was killed and Henry III was once again in control of parliament.

(B) A painting of Henry III (c. 1308)

When Edward I (1272 to 1307) was king he was constantly short of money. The main reason for this was that he was involved in fighting wars in Wales, Scotland and France.

In the past king's had concentrated on obtaining money from their tenants-in-chief. They in turn collected money from people who farmed the land on their estates. However, by the end of the 13th century, some of the richest people in the country were merchants living in the towns and most of them did not own much land.

In 1275 Edward called a meeting of parliament. As well as his tenants-in-chief, Edward, like Simon de Montfort before him, invited representatives

(C) Margaret Paston, extract from a letter to her husband. (21 October, 1460)
You have the prayers of the poor people that God should speed you at this parliament... they live in hope that you should help to set a way that they might live in better peace.

(D) Woodcut of Edward I (c. 1500).

from every shire and town in England. At the parliament Edward explained about his need for money. He must have argued his case well as parliament agreed that people should pay the king a fifteenth of all their movable property. Parliament also agreed a custom duty of 6s 8d on each sack of wool exported. The representatives then had the job of going back home and persuading the people in their area to pay these taxes.

Whenever the king needed money he called another parliament. Towns often had difficulty finding people willing to attend. They also had the problem of raising the money needed to send their representatives to the meeting. Some towns ignored the king's request and refused to send people to parliament. However, even when they did this, they still had to pay the taxes that were agreed at the meeting.

When the representatives arrived they usually met in five different groups: (1) the prelates (bishops and abbots); (2) the magnates (earls and barons); (3) the inferior clergy; (4) the knights from the shires; (5) the citizens from the towns.

As soon as agreement was reached about taxes, groups 3, 4 and 5 (the commons) were sent home. The king would then discuss issues such as new laws with his bishops, abbots, earls and barons (the lords).

C12:1 How did parliaments after 1264 differ from the councils held by kings in the early Middle Ages? (AT1 L3c)

C12:2 Select two sources from this unit that help to explain why the Commons in Parliament were sometimes reluctant to grant the king the taxes that he wanted. (AT3 L4)

C12:3 Give as many reasons as you can why kings like Edward I held regular parliaments. Explain which one of these reasons was the most important. (AT1 L6b)

C12:4 Study all the sources in this unit. How valuable would these sources be for a historian studying the early history of Parliament? (AT3 L6) What would a historian want to know about these sources before deciding their value as information on the early history of Parliament? (AT3 L7)

(E) Report of a meeting of Parliament in 1376.
In the year 1376 King Edward III held his parliament in London... Sir John Knyvet, the Chancellor of England described how the realm was in peril and on the point of being destroyed by France, Spain, Gascony, Flanders, Scotland, and other nations, by land and by sea. Sir John asked on the king's behalf for aid against his enemies... A knight of the south country rose and went to the reading desk in the centre of the chapter house... "Gentlemen... it seems to me that this is too much to grant, for the commons are so impoverished by the taxes which we have granted for a long time... we have lost... because it has been badly wasted and falsely spent... Our lord king should live and govern the kingdom and maintain the war with his own revenues without demanding money from loyal subjects"... To this they all agreed.

13 : Edward I in Wales

When the Normans invaded in 1066 they were only able to conquer the area that is today known as England. For a long while Wales, Scotland and Ireland retained their independence from the Normans.

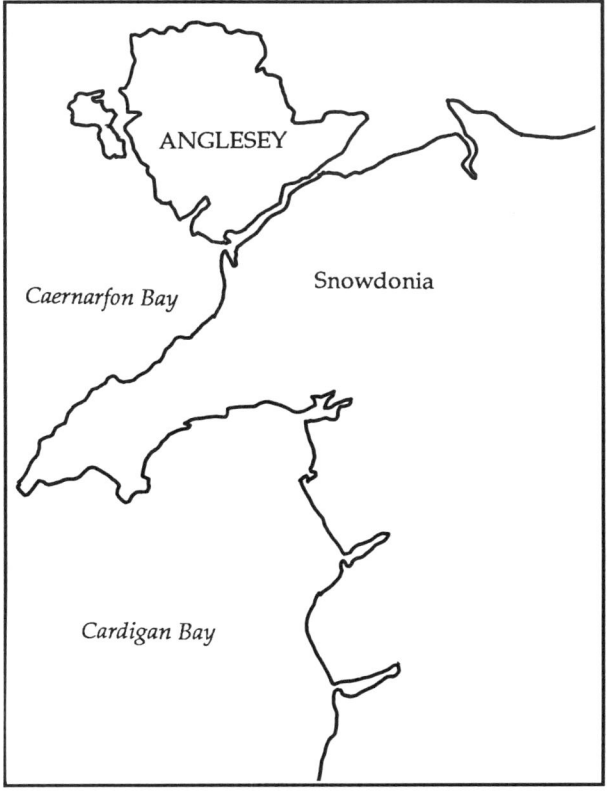

(A) Territory under the control of Llywelyn ap Gruffud in 1267.

At the time of the Norman invasion, Wales was a collection of small kingdoms without stable borders. Tenants-in-chief who had land on the borders were encouraged by the Norman kings to expand into Wales. These Normans, who became known as marcher lords, tried to do this, but the mountainous territory and the fighting abilities of the Welsh made it very difficult.

While the marcher lords won land in the east and south, North Wales remained under the control of Welsh princes. In the 13th century one of these Welsh princes, Llywelyn the Great of Gwynedd, managed to unite large areas of Wales under his control. His grandson, Llywelyn ap Gruffyd, was also successful in this policy and managed to become lord over most Welsh chieftains. In 1267 Henry III was forced to acknowledge the power of Llywelyn and granted him the title, Prince of Wales.

When Edward I became king he was determined to incorporate Wales into his kingdom. Although Llywelyn accepted that Edward was his overlord, he insisted that he should rule independently of the king.

In 1276 Edward decided to take action against Llywelyn. By cutting off the island of Anglesey, Llywelyn's main

(B) Henry II, letter to Emperor Emanuel of Constantinople (c. 1170)
In a certain part of the island there is a people called the Welsh. They are so bold and ferocious, that when unarmed, they do not fear to encounter an armed force.

(C) Manuscript painting showing Edward I and his son in 1301. (c. 1350)

(D) Manuscript painting showing Llywelyn ap Gruffyd trying to escape from the Tower of London in 1244. (c. 1250)

(E) Gerald of Wales, *Description of Wales* (c. 1195)
Their mode of fighting consists in chasing the enemy or in retreating. This light-armed people, relying more on their activity than on their strength... The defence of their native land and liberty is their sole concern: they fight for fatherland and they labour for liberty.

source of food, Edward was able to achieve victory. Llywelyn was forced to pay homage to Edward and lost all lands outside Snowdonia and Anglesey.

Llywelyn's brother, Dafydd, refused to accept this humiliating peace treaty and in 1282 he led a rebellion against Edward. After Dafydd's initial success, Llywelyn also took up arms against the English.

Edward raised a massive army against the Welsh. At one time there were over 30,000 English soldiers in Wales. Unfortunately for the Welsh, they lost both their leaders in a short space of time. Llywelyn was killed by a group of English soldiers who tricked him into believing they intended to change sides. Soon after Llywelyn's death, Dafydd was also captured and executed.

(F) Caernarvon Castle in 1990.

(G) Beaumaris Castle in 1990.

(H) Lodewyk van Veltham describing Welsh mercenaries. (c. 1305)
In the very depth of winter they were running about bare-legged... They could not have been warm... I never saw them wearing armour... Their weapons were bows, arrows and swords... They damaged the Flemings very much.

(I) Monk of Malmesbury, *Life of Edward II* (c. 1375)
The Welsh habit of revolt against the English is a long-standing madness... And this is the reason. The Welsh, formerly called the Britons, once ruled over the whole realm of England; but they were expelled by the Saxons.

(J) R. R. Davies, *Wales 1063-1415* (1987)
The Welsh simply did not have the resources to sustain a national revolt. An amateur army of peasants and labourers could not ignore the seasonal demands of cultivation. The Welsh lacked sea-power... They lacked siege-engines; they lacked the provisions to sustain a long siege.

Gradually Edward was able to gain control, and in 1284 he passed the Statute of Wales. Under the terms of the act the whole of Wales was passed over to the king. Wales was then divided into shires and ruled in the same way as England. To emphasise his dominance over the area, in 1301 Edward gave the title, the Prince of Wales, to his son.

To retain control over the area Edward ordered the building of eight castles in North Wales. They were so well-built that many of them are still in good condition today.

C13:1 Why are Llywelyn the Great of Gwynedd and Llywelyn ap Gruffyd both important figures in Welsh history? (AT1 L3b)

C13:2 Study sources A and J. Explain why Edward's tactics against Prince Llywelyn involved stopping ships from travelling from Anglesey to the Welsh mainland. (AT3 L3)

C13:3 Which sources in this unit would provide useful information for a historian who wanted to write about Welsh resistance to English rule? (AT3 L6)

C13:4 Study source C. What do you think is taking place in this picture? Why did Edward I do this? How would the Welsh people have reacted to this event? (AT1 L6c)

14 : The Struggle for Scotland

The Normans were never able to penetrate very deep into Scotland. As the land was considered to be fairly poor and a long way from their centre of government, the Normans eventually gave up the idea of conquering Scotland.

For the next two hundred years relations between England and Scotland tended to be fairly friendly. Occasionally English kings made claims to the territory, but little effort was made to take it by force.

In 1286 the king of Scotland, Alexander III, fell from his horse and broke his neck. Alexander's three children had already died, so his heir was his three-year-old granddaughter, the Maid of Norway. When the Queen was six years old it was agreed that she should marry the eldest son of King Edward I of England. Edward hoped that in this way his son would eventually become king of both England and Scotland. However, Edward's plan failed when in 1290 the Maid of Norway died while on the way to meet her proposed husband.

There was now a struggle for the throne of Scotland. Thirteen different people put forward their claims and Edward I was asked to decide who should be the next king of Scotland. Edward chose John Balliol. This upset

(A) Song, *The Reign of Edward I* (c. 1290)
The Scots raise their spears armed in their rags... The kilted people, numerous and savage, fell at Dunbar, and now stink like a dog. Vain glory made the deceitful people deny the true lord of Scotland... the wild people of Scotland soon break their faith... Scotland will not be obedient; it forces the king with his army to return... and reduces them to slavery... the English like angels are always conquerors.

(B) Statue of Robert Bruce at Stirling Castle.

the other claimants who argued that Edward only selected Balliol because he had a weak character and was easy to control.

This fear was justified when Edward began to undermine Balliol's power. For example, Edward announced that, in future, Scottish people could appeal to him if they were dissatisfied with decisions made by their king.

In 1296, under pressure from his powerful lords, John Balliol told Edward that he was renouncing the homage that he had made to him. Edward was furious and demanded that John Balliol meet him in Berwick, Scotland's main trading centre. When the Scottish king did not turn up, Edward's army killed about 13,000 people who lived in the town. Edward ordered that the dead were not be buried but had to be left

> **(C) Matthew of Westminster, *Flowers of History* (c. 1310)**
> William Wallace, a man void of pity, a robber given to arson and murder, more hardened in cruelty than Herod, more raging in madness than Nero... was condemned to a most cruel but justly deserved death. He was drawn through the streets of London at the tails of horses, until he reached a gallows... especially prepared for him; there he was suspended on a halter; but taken down while alive, he was mutilated, his bowels torn out and burned in a fire, his head then cut off, his body divided into four, and his quarters transmitted to four principal parts of Scotland.

lying in the streets as a warning to others.

When he heard the news, John Balliol surrendered, but many Scots were unwilling to accept Edward as their king. In 1297, William Wallace led a rebellion against the English. His most famous victory was at Stirling Bridge, where Scottish infantrymen were able to defeat a large English army of mounted knights. Wallace continued to create problems for the English army until he was captured in 1305 and executed for treason.

(D) Statue of Robert Bruce at Bannockburn.

The following year Robert Bruce became the new leader of Scotland's resistance to English rule. Bruce avoided pitched battles and instead relied on guerrilla warfare. His tactics against the English were very successful and Edward had to concentrate on holding on to a few of the main towns and castles in Scotland.

After the death of Edward I the war continued to go badly for England. Bruce took castle after castle and eventually only Stirling was left in English control.

In 1314 Bruce besieged Stirling castle. In an attempt to save the castle Edward II decided to march north with the largest army that had ever left England. Bruce was waiting for him, and at Bannockburn, just south of Stirling, Edward's army of 23,000 men suffered a terrible defeat. Although outnumbered, Scotland's foot-soldiers had beaten England's mounted knights.

Bruce now controlled Scotland and in 1320 he issued the Declaration of Arbroath. The declaration ended with the words: "for as long as a hundred of us remain alive, we will never on any condition be subjected to the lordship of

> **(E) Andreas Franciscius, *Journey to England* (1497)**
> The whole island is divided into two parts, one of which is called England, and the other, in the north, Scotland. At the head of Scotland is a King who rules very fierce and courageous tribes, who are always the enemies of the English, and very frequently at war with them.

(F) Painting of Robert Bruce and Elizabeth de Burgh that appeared in a book in 1591.

C14:1 Place the following events in the order in which they happened, and then explain how they are connected. (a) The Maid of Norway dies on the way to meet Prince Edward; (b) Marriage arranged between the Maid of Norway and Prince Edward; (c) John Balliol becomes king of Scotland; (d) Alexander III dies after falling from a horse. (AT1 L5c)

C14:2 Make a time-line dated 1280-1330. On the time-line include the important events that help to illustrate the relationship between England and Scotland during this period. (AT1 L4c)

C14:3 What are the advantages and disadvantages of the following sources to a historian writing about the conflict between England and Scotland: (a) accounts written by foreign visitors such as sources E and G; (b) paintings of famous people such as source F? (AT3 L6)

C14:4 Writers sometimes attempt to influence the opinions of the reader by the adjectives they use. Give examples of how the writers of sources A and C use language to influence their readers. (AT2 L6)

C14:5 Sources B and D are two modern portraits of Robert Bruce. Every day hundreds of tourists see these sculptures at Stirling Castle and Bannockburn. It has been claimed that these sculptures are works of propaganda. Do you agree? It will help if you look up the term propaganda in *Source Material Key Words*. (AT2 L7)

the English." For a while it looked as though England was willing to accept defeat, and in 1328 Edward III recognised Scottish independence and Robert Bruce's right to be king by signing the Treaty of Edinburgh.

However, despite signing this treaty Edward III, like his father and grandfather before him, was determined to conquer Scotland. After Bruce died of leprosy in 1329, Edward III launched another attack on Scotland. Although Edward III won an important victory over King David II (Robert Bruce's son) at Haildon Hill in 1333, the continued use of guerrilla tactics made it impossible for the English army to subdue the Scots. With the costs of fighting the war creating problems with tax-payers in England, Edward III eventually decided to withdraw from Scotland.

(G) Jean Froissart, *Chronicles* (c. 1395)
The Scots are tough and very bold and active in the use of arms and in fighting. Their opinion of the English was low, as it still is to the present day... The Scottish men are right hardy, and good travellers in armour and in war. When they come into England, they will drive their whole army 24 miles in a single day... During a war they will live for a long time on half-cooked meat, with nothing to drink but water from the rivers. Nor do they carry any pots or pans, since they cook animals in their skins... Also, behind his saddle, each man carries a broad metal plate and a little sack, full of oatmeal. After they have eaten their meat, they put this plate on the fire, and mix some oatmeal with water.

15 : The Medieval Village Economy

Around most medieval villages there were three large arable fields. Two of these fields grew crops while the third was left fallow. The village would also have hay meadows and common land where the peasants had the right to graze their animals.

The three arable fields were divided into strips, each one being separated from the next by balks of unploughed land. To ensure that everybody had a fair share of the good land, each family was given strips in all three fields.

These strips were long and narrow because the peasants wanted to reduce to a minimum the number of times the plough-team had to turn round. On light soils a pair of oxen could successfully pull a plough. However, heavy clay soils needed a team of eight oxen. As most peasants only owned about two oxen they would have to join with others in order to have their land ploughed.

Medieval farmers preferred oxen to horses because they were less expensive to feed, stronger on heavy land and could be eaten when they died. The plough they used had an iron-tipped coulter in front to make the initial cut and a mould board to turn the soil over in a furrow. The fields were ploughed three times: the first turned the stubble over, the second removed the thistles and weeds and the third prepared the ground for sowing.

(A) Engraving by Peter Bruegel (c.1568)

The three-field system of crop-rotation was employed by medieval farmers, with spring as well as autumn sowings. Wheat or rye was planted in one field, and oats, barley, peas, lentils or broad beans were planted in the second field. The third field was left fallow. Each year the crops were rotated

(B) The three-field system of crop rotation			
	1st year	2nd year	3rd year
1st field	autumn planting (wheat, rye)	spring planting (wheat, oats, barley, beans)	fallow
2nd field	spring planting (wheat, oats, barley, beans)	fallow	autumn planting (wheat, rye)
3rd field	fallow	autumn planting (wheat, rye)	spring planting (wheat, oats, barley, beans)

(C) Painting in Queen Mary's Psalter (c. 1320)

to leave one field fallow. This system also ensured that the same crop was not grown in the same field two years running.

Medieval farmers did what they could to increase the fertility of the land. They were aware that the soil would only give back as much as was put into it. Marl (a mixture of clay and carbonate of lime) and seaweed were used as fertilisers. Farmers knew that the best fertiliser was animal dung. However, small farmers could not afford the cost of feeding large numbers of animals and so manure was often in short supply.

The timing of the harvest in the Middle Ages was vitally important. If the wheat was too dry the grain would fall off. If it was too wet the grain would rot. To ensure that his own crops did not go to waste, the lord of the manor could demand extra labour services called boon-work during harvest time.

(D) Part of a song performed by medieval minstrels, *The Husbandman Song* (c. 1360)
To find money for the king I sold my seed.
Wherefore my land lies fallow and learns to sleep..

(E) *Chronicle of Bury St Edmunds* (1258)
There was a great shortage of everything because of the floods of the previous year, and corn, which was very scarce, cost from 15 shillings to as much as 20 shillings a quarter. Famine resulted so that the poor had to eat horse-meat, the bark of trees and even more unpleasant things. Many died of hunger.

(F) Drawing in a book of hymns (c. 1020)

Boon-work was hated by the villeins as it delayed their own harvesting and could cause their own crops to be ruined.

Despite the efforts of medieval farmers, their crop yields per acre amounted to only about a fifth of those achieved by farmers today. As villeins had to give about half their crop away as rent and taxes, they needed to farm a large area of land to provide an adequate diet for themselves. People dying of starvation was not unusual in the Middle Ages. This was especially true when bad weather led to a poor harvest.

(G) Walter of Henley, *Fleta* (c. 1275)
The Reeve, elected by the village to that office as the best manager... Let him therefore not be slothful or sleepy, but let him unceasingly strive for his lord's profit... When the dung is to be carried to the fields, let the Reeve stay with the carters, that they may labour and finish their day's work without trickery... Let the threshers and winnowing-women be closely spied upon, lest they steal corn in their shoes, gloves, bags or satchels hidden near the barn.

C15:1 Look at the picture on the front cover and sources D and F on page 34. All these pictures show a harrow being used. (i) Describe a harrow. (ii) Explain what a harrow was used for. (iii) Identify two methods that medieval farmers used to stop the birds eating the seeds they planted. (AT3 L3)

C15:2 Study sources A, C and F from this unit and source G on page 35. What evidence is there in these pictures that some farming equipment in the Middle Ages changed while others stayed the same? (AT1 L4a)

C15:3 How did medieval farmers attempt to maximise the food that their land produced? (AT1 L4c)

C15:4 Give as many reasons as you can why people in the Middle Ages sometimes died of starvation. Select passages from the sources to help you answer this question. (AT3 L4)

C15:5 Study sources C and F from this unit and source D (page 34). Describe the different tasks these people are performing. What order would these tasks have been performed during the farming year? (AT1 L5c)

(H) Anonymous, *The Reign of King Stephen* (c. 1190)
In 1143... a terrible famine prevailed all over England... some, from lack of food, ate the forbidden flesh of dogs or horses... people wasted away and died in droves... You could have seen villages extremely well-known standing lonely and almost empty because the peasants of both sexes and all ages were dead.

(I) Engraving by Peter Bruegel (1563)

16 : Women in the Village Economy

Women played an important role in the village economy. As the men had to provide the labour services by working several days a week on the lord's demesne, it was the women who had to look after the family crops.

Women not only laboured in the fields. They did most of the sheep-shearing and were usually in charge of the garden where they grew vegetables and kept a few chickens. Women also made the cloth, cooked the food, and looked after the children.

As well as supplying the needs of their families, women were often involved in producing goods for sale. It was they rather than men who were more likely to produce bread, beer or clothes to be sold to other members of the village.

(A) Details of labour services at Frochester Manor. (1265)
Margery, the widow, holds 24 acres and she pays 3s every year... From Michaelmas to the Feast of St Peter she must plough half an acre every week... And from the Feast of St John the Baptist until August she must perform manual service 3 days every week... She shall mow the lord's meadow for at least 4 days... And she must lift the lord's hay for at least 4 days... She shall weed 2 days... And from the Feast of St Peter until Michaelmas she must perform manual service 5 days a week... And furthermore she performs 8 boon works in autumn... And she shall give eggs at Easter at will.

(B) Manuscript painting from a book published in about 1250.

(C) 19th century drawing based on an illustration from the Luttrell Psalter (c. 1325)

On the death of her husband, a woman was entitled by law to take over a third of his holding. In some villages, women who were able to pay the entry fees to the lord, were allowed to carry on farming all the land.

Despite the fact that women contributed so much to the village economy they did not have the same rights as men in the village. For example, women were not allowed to be appointed to official posts such as bailiff, reeve, constable or aletaster.

C16:1 Study sources B and C from this unit and sources A and C on page 33. Describe the work these women are doing. Why do you think most of these women have their heads covered? (AT3 L4)

C16:2 Select passages from the written sources in this unit to show that women worked very hard during the Middle Ages. (AT3 L4)

C16:3 What type of sources would a historian need to study if he or she wanted to write a book about the kind of work women did in the village? (AT3 L6)

C16:4 Do you think that everyone who was alive in England in, say 1340, had an equal chance of being known about today? Use your knowledge of the sources available for this period to answer this question. (AT2 L6)

C16:5 Sources D and E are both taken from books that gave advice on farming. Historians would use sources such as these to discover the kind of work that women did during the Middle Ages. Why is it difficult for a historian to obtain detailed information about the work of women from books like these? (AT2 L7)

(D) Christine de Pisan, *Three Virtues* (1406)
She (the lady of the manor) should be a good manager, knowledgeable about farming, knowing in what weather and in what season the fields should be worked... She should often take her recreation in the fields in order to see how the work is progressing, for there are many who would willingly stop raking the ground beyond the surface if they thought nobody would notice.

(E) William FitzHerbert, *Book of Husbandry* (c. 1140)
If the husband has sheep of his own, then his wife may have some of the wool, to make her husband and herself some clothes... she may also take wool to spin for the cloth makers. That way she can earn her own living, and still have plenty of time to do other work... It is the wife's occupation to winnow corn, to make malt, to wash clothes, to make hay and to cut corn. In time of need she should help her husband fill the dung-cart, drive the plough, and load the hay and corn. She should also go to the market to sell butter, cheese, milk, eggs, chickens, pigs, geese and corn. And also to buy the things needed for the household.

17 : Alice Sprout of Woolstone

Nearly all villeins were illiterate so they have not left detailed accounts of their lives. However, by studying manor records it is possible to obtain information on what life was like for individual villeins. For example, Alice Sprout lived in Woolstone, Oxfordshire. The Woolstone manor records show that Alice married Stephen Sprout in 1341.

For many years the couple farmed four acres of land in Woolstone. Later, he was elected as Woolstone's reeve. The 2 shillings per year that went with the job enabled the Sprouts to increase their holding to fifteen acres. As Stephen's job as reeve kept him fully occupied, most of the work on this land would have been done by Alice. To make a profit, Alice had to be a good farmer because the lord charged her a yearly rent of 7 shillings for the land.

The Sprouts only had one child who survived into adulthood. In 1371 the couple asked the lord of the manor if they could buy their son's freedom. The lord agreed as long as the boy was trained as a priest. As the lord was a very religious man he only charged the Sprouts 3 shillings 4 pence for the boy's freedom.

When Stephen died in 1384, Alice had to give her best two animals to the lord and the rector. Alice also had to pay an entry fee in order to carry on farming her fifteen acres. Alice Sprout continued farming for another four years, but when she reached the age of sixty she asked the lord if she could buy her freedom. The lord agreed and the manor records show that Alice had to pay 30 shillings for the right to leave the village. As this is the last time that Alice appeared in the village records, it is not known what happened to her after 1388.

C17:1 What do the Woolstone manor records tell us about the type of person Alice Sprout must have been? (AT1 L4c)

C17:2 What does source A tell us about the life of a medieval peasant? (AT3 L5) Why do we know more about the houses that rich people lived in during the Middle Ages than the houses of peasants? (AT3 L7)

(A) Re-construction of a house that a medieval peasant like Alice Sprout would have lived in.

18 : The Black Death

Death from disease was a constant fear of people living in the Middle Ages. Leprosy, smallpox, diphtheria, measles and influenza were all major killers during this period. However, it was a new disease against which people had no immunity that led to what has been described as "the worst disaster in the history of the world."

The plague (or the Black Death as it was later called) first broke out in southern China in the early 1330s. The Black Death then moved on to India. Travellers returning from this country told of how whole communities had been completely destroyed by the disease. These stories aroused terrible fears in Europe. Many people believed that the disease heralded the end of the world.

> **(A) In a letter to a friend in Rome, a Flemish priest described the outbreak of the Black Death in India. (1346)**
> On the first day there was a rain of frogs, serpents, lizards, scorpions... On the second, thunder was heard, and lightning and sheets of fire fell upon the earth, mingled with hail stones of marvellous size; which slew almost all, from the greatest to the least. On the third day there fell fire from heaven and stinking smoke, which slew all that were left of men and beasts.

The first case in England was reported in the Dorset port of Melcombe Regis in September 1348. From Dorset it spread west to Devon, Cornwall and Somerset. The port of Bristol, England's second largest town, was very badly hit. It has been estimated that approximately 40% of the town's population died from the disease.

It then started moving east. Hampshire, Sussex, Surrey and by the end of September it was in London.

(B) Manuscript painting of a leper (c.1400)

When the disease hit an area there was a strong temptation for people to flee. This created hostility from people living in other towns and villages who feared that the new arrivals would bring the disease with them.

(C) Woodcut from a book called *Dance of Death* published in 1492.

(D) Henry Knighton, *Chronicle*, (c. 1395)

Many villages and hamlets became deserted... Sheep and cattle went wandering over fields and through crops and there was no one to go and look after them... In the following autumn no one could get a reaper for less than 8d. with his food, a mower for less than 12d. with his food. Therefore, many crops perished in the fields for want of someone to gather them.

The first symptoms of the Black Death included a high temperature, tiredness, shivering and pains all over the body. The next stage was the appearance of small red boils on the neck, in the armpit or groin. These lumps, called buboes, grew larger and darker in colour. Eyewitness accounts talk of these buboes growing to the size of apples. The final stage of the illness was the appearance of small, red spots on the stomach and other parts of the body. This was caused by internal bleeding, and death followed soon after.

(E) Woodcut *The Child* (c. 1524)

(F) Woodcut from a book called *How to Die* (c. 1450)

The Black Death is, in fact, not one but two related diseases. The most common form is bubonic plague. This disease is spread when infected fleas that normally live on black rats land on people and bite them. A person suffering from bubonic plague in the Middle Ages had a 60% chance of dying within two to five days of being infected.

In some cases bubonic plague becomes concentrated in the lungs and causes symptoms similar to pneumonia. This pneumonic version is even worse than bubonic plague. People with pneumonic plague usually die within a couple of hours of catching the disease. It is also highly infectious, as people can catch it by breathing in bacilli coughed out by the person suffering from the disease.

Doctors could do little to help those suffering from the Black Death. The most common form of treatment was to lance the buboes, expelling a foul-smelling, blackish liquid. Other methods involved bleeding and washing the body with vinegar.

> **(G) Giovanni Boccaccio, *Decameron* (c. 1360)**
> It first betrayed itself by the emergence of certain tumours in the groin or the armpits, some of which grew as large as a common apple, others as an egg... merely by speech or association with the sick was the disease communicated to the healthy... any that touched the clothes of the sick... seemed to catch the disease... Many died daily or nightly in the public streets. Of many others, who died at home, the departure was hardly observed by their neighbours, until the stench of the bodies carried the news.

People also took preventive measures. As they believed that God was all powerful, they assumed that praying would help. They also looked very carefully at their behaviour to see if they could discover why God was so angry with them. The priests gave several reasons for the Black Death. They claimed that peasants did not show enough respect for the clergy, drank and swore too much, and did not spend enough time praying. Some priests even put the Black Death down to too much dancing and having long hair.

It was believed that one way of avoiding the plague was to punish yourself for your sins before you caught the disease. People took part in what became known as "flagellant processions". This involved people whipping each other in public.

Some priests claimed that the Black Death was a sign from God that the world was coming to an end. It was therefore people's last chance to change their behaviour if they wanted to obtain a place in heaven. Other people took the opposite view. If death was likely to occur soon, why not enjoy yourself while you were still alive? The moral behaviour of people who took this view declined rather than improved during this period.

(I) Woodcut from a book published in about 1480.

> **(H) The Bishop of Bath, wrote a letter about the Black Death to all the priests in his diocese. (January 1349)**
> The plague... has left many parish churches... without parson or priest to care for their parishioners... Therefore, to provide for the salvation of souls... you should at once publicly command and persuade all men that, if they are on the point of death and cannot secure the services of a priest, then they should make confession to each other... if no man is present, then even to a woman.

C18:1 Describe what is taking place in sources B, C, E, F and I. (AT3 L3)

C18:2 Make a list of the different things people thought caused the Black Death. Select passages from the sources to help you answer this question. (AT1 L4c)

C18:3 Did the outbreak of the Black Death cause local, national or international changes? (AT1 L5a)

C18:4 How useful are sources A, C, D and I to a historian writing a book on the outbreak of the Black Death in Britain in 1348? (AT3 L6)

C18:5 Between 1348 and 1375 there were several outbreaks of plague. As a result of these outbreaks, historians believe that the population of Britain fell from 4.2 million to 2.2 million. What kind of effect do you think this dramatic fall in population had on Britain? Give as many examples as you can. It will help if you consider issues such as work, wages, taxation and religion. (AT1 L7a)

19 : The Peasants' Revolt

In May 1381, Thomas Bampton, the Tax Commissioner for the Essex area, reported to the king that the people of Fobbing were refusing to pay their poll tax. It was decided to send a Chief Justice and a few soldiers to the village. It was thought that if a few of the ringleaders were executed the rest of the village would be frightened into paying the tax.

However, when the Chief Justice arrived, he was attacked by the villagers. He was captured and forced to sign a document promising not to take any further part in the collection of the poll tax. After releasing the Chief Justice, some of the villagers looted and set fire to the home of John Sewale, the Sheriff of Essex. The people responsible hid in the woods and sent out messages to the villages of Essex and Kent asking for their support in the fight against the poll tax.

Many peasants decided that it was time to support the ideas proposed by John Ball and his followers. It was not long before Wat Tyler, a former soldier in the Hundred Years War, emerged as the leader of the peasants.

(B) Rolls of Parliament (1380)
The lords and commons are agreed that... three groats should be given from each lay person of the realm... who have reached the age of fifteen.

Tyler's first decision was to march to Maidstone to free John Ball from prison. The peasants then moved on to Canterbury. Here they took over the archbishop's palace, destroyed legal documents and released prisoners from Canterbury prison.

News of the rebellion spread all over Essex and Kent. More and more peasants decided to take action. Manor houses were broken into and documents were destroyed. These records included the villeins' names, the rent they paid and the services they carried out. What had originally started as a protest against the poll tax now became an attempt to destroy the feudal system.

The peasants decided to go to London to see King Richard II. As Richard was only fourteen they blamed his advisers for the poll tax. The peasants hoped that once the king knew about their problems, he would do something to solve them.

(A) Painting of Richard II (c. 1396)

(C) Extract from a poem (c. 1381)
A man with goods worth forty pounds has to pay twelve round pence. And another, brought to the ground by poverty, has to pay as much.

(D) Henry Knighton, *Chronicle* (c. 1395)
The rebels returned to the New Temple which belonged to the prior of Clerkenwell... and tore up with their axes all the church books, charters and records discovered in the chests and burnt them... One of the criminals chose a fine piece of silver and hid it in his lap; when his fellows saw him carrying it, they threw him, together with his prize, into the fire, saying they were lovers of truth and justice, not robbers and thieves.

The rebels reached the outskirts of the city on 12 June. It has been estimated that approximately 30,000 peasants had marched to London. At Blackheath, John Ball gave one of his famous sermons on the need for "freedom and equality". Wat Tyler also spoke to the rebels. He told them: "Remember, we come not as thieves and robbers. We come seeking social justice."

Richard II gave orders for the peasants to be locked out of London. However some Londoners who sympathised with the peasants arranged for the city gates to be left open. When the rebels entered the city, Richard II and his advisers withdrew to the Tower of London.

Many poor people living in London

(E) Thomas Walsingham, *English History* (c. 1395)
They set out for the residence of the duke of Lancaster... They tore the golden cloths and silk hangings to pieces and crushed them underfoot; they ground up rings and other jewels inlaid with precious stones so that they could not be used again.

decided to join the rebellion. Together they began to destroy the property of the king's senior officials. After a while, in an attempt to stop the rioting, Richard II decided to meet the rebels at Mile End. When he arrived the king was handed a petition which asked for the abolition of serfdom, the right to sell their labour,

(F) 19th century engraving of John Ball and the peasants entering London. The engraving is a copy of a painting that appeared in a book published in 1460.

> **(G) *Chronicle of St Mary's* (1381)**
> And the king said to Wat Tyler: "Why will you not go back to your own county?" Wat Tyler answered that neither he nor his fellows would leave until they had got their charter as they wished to have it... And he demanded that there should be only one bishop in England... and all the lands and possessions (of the church) should be taken from them and divided among the commons... And he demanded that there should be no more villeins in England, and no serfdom... that all men should be free.

> **(I) Charter issued by Richard II in 1381 to the peasants of Hertford.**
> Subjects and others of the county of Hertford, freed each and all of their old bondage... pardoned them all felonies, treasons, and extortions committed by any and all of them.

a fixed rent of four pence per acre and a pardon for any crimes committed during the uprising.

Richard II agreed to these proposals and 30 clerks were instructed to write out charters giving peasants their freedom. When they received their charters, the peasants began to go home to their villages.

While Richard II was in Mile End, another group of peasants marched to the Tower of London. There were about 600 soldiers defending the Tower but they decided not to fight the rebel army. Simon Sudbury (Archbishop of Canterbury), Robert Hales (King's Treasurer) and John Legge (Tax Commissioner), were taken from the Tower and executed. Their heads were then placed on poles and paraded through the streets of cheering Londoners.

The next day, Richard II met the rebels at Smithfield. Wat Tyler rode over to the king and put forward another list of demands that included: the removal of the lordship system, the distribution of the wealth of the church to the poor, a reduction in the number of bishops, and a guarantee that in future there would be no more villeins.

Richard II said he would do what he could. Wat Tyler was not satisfied by this reply. He called for a drink of water to rinse out his mouth. This was seen as extremely rude behaviour, especially as Tyler had not removed his hood when talking to the king. One of Richard's party shouted out that Tyler was "the greatest thief and robber in Kent". Tyler drew his dagger and, in the scuffle that followed, Tyler was badly wounded.

(H) The death of the Archbishop of Canterbury. This illustration appeared in a 1460 edition of Frossiart's *Chronicles*.

> **(J) Jean Froissart, *Chronicles* (c. 1395)**
> Then the king ordered thirty clerks to write letters, sealed with his seal. And when the people received the letters, they went back home. But Wat Tyler, Jack Straw and John Ball said they would not leave. More than 30,000 stayed with them. They were in no hurry to have the King's letters. They meant to slay all the rich people of London and rob their homes.

(K) 19th century engraving of King Richard talking to the peasants at Smithfield.

The peasants raised their weapons and for a moment it looked as though there was going to be fighting between the king's soldiers and the peasants. However, Richard rode over to them and said: "Will you shoot your king?" He then spoke to them for some time and eventually they agreed to go back to their villages.

Meanwhile, Wat Tyler had been taken to St. Bartholomew's Hospital. He was not there long when the king's officials arrived and killed him. Other rebel leaders such as John Ball were also executed.

(L) Michael Senior, *Richard II* (1981)
It (Wat Tyler's character) is not a pleasant sight, and Richard undoubtedly benefits by comparison. But history is not written by peasants... One would expect Tyler to have had a bad press... but those reports, however partial, are all we have to go on.

(M) William Grindcobbe was the leader of the rebellion in St Albans. Soon after this speech he was captured and executed (quoted in Walsingham's *Chronicle*).
Friends, who after so long an age of oppression, have at last won yourselves a short breath of freedom, hold firm while you can, and have no thought for me or what I may suffer. For if I die for the cause of liberty that we have won, I shall think myself happy to end my life as a martyr.

(N) Richard II talking to peasants in Essex after the revolt. (1381)
You who are not worthy to live when compared with the lords whom you have attacked... You were and are serfs, and shall remain in bondage, but in one infinitely worse.

C19:1 Read sources B and C. How do these sources help to explain why some peasants disliked the poll tax? (AT1 L3b)

C19:2 Study sources I and N. Explain why Richard II changed his mind on the subject of feudalism. (AT1 L3a)

C19:3 It has been claimed that the Peasants' revolt was an attempt to bring an end to the feudal system. Select passages from the sources in this unit that supports this view. (AT3 L4)

C19:4 How reliable is the information in source J. It will help you to read the other sources in this unit before answering this question. (AT2 L5)

C19:5 The main sources of information on the Peasants' Revolt come from the writings of Henry Knighton, Thomas Walsingham and Jean Froissart. Read about these men on pages 67 and 68 and then explain the point being made by Michael Senior in source L. (AT2 L7)

C19:6 Give as many reasons as you can why the peasants revolted in 1381. As well as the information in this unit you should also consider material that appeared in *The Feudal System, The Origins of Parliament, Economic Consequences of the Black Death, Taxation in the Middle Ages, The Poll Tax, John Ball,* and *The Lollards*. Put these reasons into the following categories: (i) economic; (ii) political; (iii) religious; (iv) individual. (AT1 L7b)

20 : Towns and Trade

When the Normans arrived in England nearly everyone lived in villages, hamlets and isolated farmsteads. However, in time some of these villages grew into towns.

Villages usually developed into towns for geographical reasons. Sometimes it was because a village was the site of a good harbour (Southampton, Dover, Plymouth), sometimes because it was a good place to cross a river (Chelmsford, Oxford, Cambridge).

Towns also developed where two important roads crossed (Winchester, Salisbury, Huntingdon). Places such as these were guaranteed a steady stream of travellers. For people with things to sell, this was a good place to be.

Towns, like villages, were usually owned by the local lord. He encouraged the growth of the town because it meant more money for him. He charged people for having stalls in the market or for bringing goods into the town.

(A) Charter issued in 1270
We have granted to the barons of Pevensey that they may have there every year a fair to continue for seven days... and a market on every Sunday, provided that the fair and market shall not be a nuisance to the neighbouring fairs and markets.

(C) Woodcut published in about 1490.

It was not long before these towns had large groups of skilled workers such as carpenters, tailors, shoemakers, saddlers, blacksmiths, weavers, fullers and dyers. These workers often organised themselves into craft guilds. At first all the people involved in a particular trade joined the same guild. The main purpose of these guilds was to protect the interests of their members. This included maintaining the quality of goods produced in the town by that trade. Guilds also tried to restrict

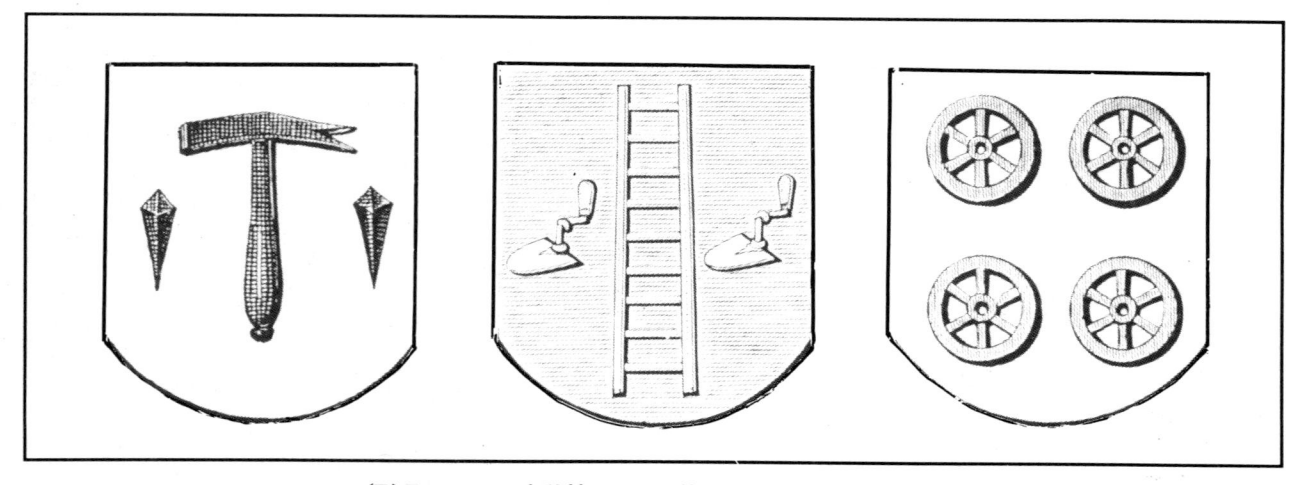

(B) Banners of different guilds during the Middle Ages.

> **(D) Order issued by Bristol Weavers in 1461.**
> Many weavers in the town of Bristol... hire their wives, daughters and maidens to weave in their own looms... and men are unoccupied and cannot labour... therefore, no person of the Bristol craft of weavers from this day forward, may hire his wife, daughter or maid to such occupation of weaving... upon pain of 6s. 8d.

competition by stopping non-members from trading in the town, and by controlling the number of apprentices who could be trained.

At first these skilled workers tended to be self-employed. However, in time, some began to employ others to work for them. This created a conflict of interest between the masters and their employees. For example, masters wanted to keep wages low while the workers wanted them to be high.

By the 14th century merchants in certain trades began to form themselves into organisations called mercantile guilds. The people who worked for these merchants also formed their own guilds (sometimes known as brotherhoods) in an attempt to increase their wages and to improve their working conditions.

People in towns also formed confraternities which provided a form of social insurance. Membership of confraternities varied. Some were restricted to people who worked in a particular trade, while membership of others depended on where people lived. Each week members of a confraternity paid money into a fund. This fund was then used to help members who were not able to work due to illness, injury or old age.

(E) Engraving of a fair held at Hoboken in the Netherlands. (1559)

(F) Market traders (1519)

(G) *Chronicle of London* (1396)
There had been much strife between the masters of the trade of saddlers and their journeymen. The masters complained that the journeymen were... holding meetings... both outside and within the city... Under cover of religion, many of the journeyman had formed secret organisations with the object of raising wages. In the past, a master could have had a journeyman for £2 a year. Now such a man would not agree to work for less than £10 a year.

To raise money, kings began to allow towns to buy themselves a degree of independence. To do this they had to buy a charter from the king. These charters gave people the right to a certain amount of self-government. The people would meet in the market-square, and after proposals were put, people would shout either "yea" or "nay".

However, as the towns grew it was the wealthy merchants who gradually took control of government. Sometimes

(H) Thaxted Guild Hall built in about 1390.

the rich took advantage of their power by imposing heavy taxes on the poor. This created a great deal of bad feeling and there were occasions when the king was forced to intervene to stop unfair taxes being imposed on the people living in towns.

(I) Taxes in the city of Winchester (c. 1275)
Every cart bringing fish for sale into the city pays a halfpenny to the king's rent...
Every seller of herrings is to pay 6d to the king, and a pitcher of wine to the bailiffs...
Butchers who keep a stall, is to pay to the king, 25d. per annum...
All persons who bring cattle, sheep, or pigs, and sell them alive, are to pay 5d. a year to the king... and to the city clerk, 1d., for enrolling their names...
Every baker of bread for sale is charged 2d. per annum to the king, and 1d. to the city clerk... Every baker is to have his known seal on the bread.

(J) Drawing published in about 1450.

C20:1 Study sources B, C, J and L. Which crafts do you think are represented in these pictures? (AT3 L3)

C20:2 Study source I on page 36. Describe the different games the children are playing. How many of these games are still played today? (AT1 L4a)

C20:3 Study sources A, E, F and I. Explain why you think some towns held fairs in the Middle Ages. (AT3 L4) Compare the value of these sources to the historian studying fairs in England during the 13th century. (AT3 L6)

C20:4 Who joined craft guilds in the Middle Ages? Why did the membership of these guilds sometimes change while others remained the same? (AT1 L4a)

C20:5 If you were a historian writing a book on guilds, what kind of sources would you be interested in studying? Comment on the value of these sources to the historian. Consider issues such as reliability and bias. (AT3 L7)

(K) Court order issued in London (c. 1380)
The said John Penrose shall drink a draught of the same wine which he sold to the common people, and the remainder of such wine shall be poured on the head of the same John, and he shall lose the right to call himself vintner in the city of London for ever.

(L) Woodcut by Durer (1525)

21 : The Wars of the Roses

In 1453 Henry VI suffered his first bout of mental illness. Richard, duke of York, Britain's most powerful noble, was temporarily made protector of the realm. Henry's family, the Lancastrians, did not like this decision. Eventually this dispute led to armed warfare between the two sides. Known as the Wars of the Roses because of their family badges (the red rose of Lancaster and the white rose of York), this conflict was to last for thirty years.

The victory won by the Yorkists at the Battle of Towton, enabled them to provide the next two kings of England, Edward IV and Richard III. However, the Lancastrians refused to accept defeat and continued to plot the overthrow of the Yorkist kings.

In August 1485, Henry Tudor, the leader of the Lancastrians, arrived in Wales with 2,000 of his supporters. He also brought with him over 2,000 mercenaries recruited from French prisons. While in Wales, Henry also persuaded many skillful longbowmen

(B) Drawing of Henry VII (c. 1550)

to join him in his fight against Richard III. By the time Henry Tudor reached England the size of his army had grown to 5,000 men.

When Richard heard about the arrival of Henry he marched his army to meet his rival for the throne. On the way, Richard tried to recruit as many men as possible to fight in his army, but by the time he reached Leicester he only had an army of 6,000 men. The earl of Northumberland also brought 3,000 men but his loyalty to Richard was in doubt.

Richard sent an order to Lord Thomas Stanley and Sir William Stanley, two of the most powerful men

(A) Painting of Richard III (c. 1610)

(C) *The Ballad of Bosworth* **(c. 1490)**
He said, 'Give me my battle-axe in my hand,
Set the crown of England on my head so high!
For by him that shaped both sea and land,
King of England this day will die!'

```
         N  ↑   to
            |   Ashby de la Zouche      to
            |                           Leicester ↗
         ↑
            ┌──────────────┐
            │ Lord Stanley │
            └──────────────┘

                    Ambien Hill
                                 ┌──────────────┐
                                 │ King Richard │
            ┌──────────────┐     └──────────────┘
            │ Henry Tudor  │
            └──────────────┘


                   ┌────────────────┐
                   │ Sir W. Stanley │
                   └────────────────┘
                                  to
                                  Hickley ↘
```

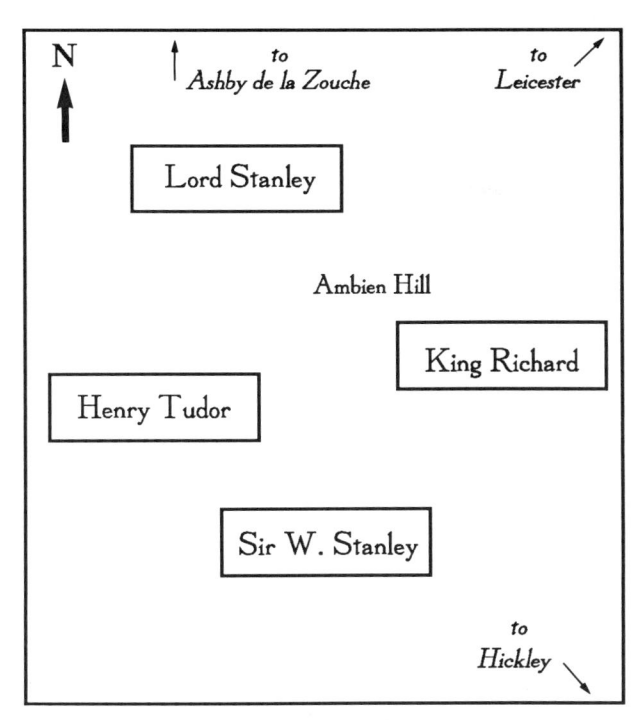

(D) Troop positions at the Battle of Bosworth

in England, to bring their 6,000 soldiers to fight for the king. Richard had been informed that Lord Stanley had already promised to help Henry Tudor. In order to persuade him to change his mind, Richard arranged for Lord Stanley's eldest son to be kidnapped.

On 21 August 1485, King Richard's army positioned themselves on Ambien Hill, close to the small village of Bosworth in Leicestershire. Henry arrived the next day and took up a position facing Richard. When the Stanley brothers arrived they did not join either of the two armies. Instead, Lord Stanley went to the north of the battlefield and Sir William to the south. The four armies now made up the four sides of a square.

> **(E) Polydore Vergil, *English History* (c. 1530)**
> Richard, because he expected victory, received Henry with great courage... Henry's army... were now almost out of hope of victory, when William Stanley with three thousand men came to the rescue... Richard's army fled, and King Richard alone was killed fighting manfully in the thickest press of his enemies.

> **(F) *The Croyland Chronicle* (1485)**
> King Richard received many mortal wounds and, like a spirited and most courageous prince, fell in battle on the field and not in flight.

Without the support of the Stanley brothers, Richard looked certain to be defeated. Richard therefore gave orders for Lord Stanley's son to be brought to the top of the hill. The king then sent a message to Lord Stanley threatening to execute his son unless he immediately sent his troops to join the king on Ambien Hill. Lord Stanley's reply was short: "Sire, I have other sons."

Henry Tudor's forces now charged King Richard's army. Although outnumbered, Richard's superior position at the top of the hill enabled him to stop the rival forces breaking through at first.

(G) A 19th century engraving of the Battle of Bosworth.

(H) John Rous, *History of England* (c. 1490)

King Richard, after receiving many mortal wounds, died a fearless and most courageous death, fighting on the battlefield, not in flight. His body was found among the other dead... and after suffering many humiliations, it was taken to Leicester in an inhuman manner, with a rope around its neck.

When the situation began to deteriorate, Richard called up his reserve forces led by the earl of Northumberland. However, Northumberland, convinced that Richard was going to lose, ignored the order.

Richard's advisers told him that he must try to get away. Richard refused, claiming that he could still obtain victory by killing Henry Tudor. He argued that once the pretender to the throne was dead, his army would have no reason to go on fighting.

A few of his close friends agreed to accompany him on his mission. So that everyone knew who he was, Richard put on his crown. After choosing an axe as his weapon, Richard and a small group of men charged down the hill.

Henry's guards quickly surrounded their leader. Before Richard could get to Henry, he was knocked off his horse. Surrounded by the enemy, Richard continued to fight until he was killed.

Tradition has it that Richard's crown was found under a gorse bush. Lord Stanley, whose intervention had proved so important, was given the honour of crowning Henry VII the new king of England and Wales.

The following year, Henry VII married Elizabeth of York, the daughter of Edward IV. In doing so, Henry united the Lancaster and York families and ensured that the Wars of the Roses were over.

(I) A sculpture of Henry VII (c. 1513)

C21:1 Read about Henry VI, Edward IV, Richard III and Henry VII on the sheet *The Kings of England 1066 to 1509*. Then make a time-line dated 1450 to 1500. Mark in important events concerning the conflict between the Lancastrians and Yorkists. (AT1 L4c)

C21:2 Study sources C, E, F and H. What impression do these sources give of Richard III at the Battle of Bosworth? (AT3 L4)

C21:3 Explain the short-term and long-term causes of Richard III's defeat at the Battle of Bosworth. (AT1 L5b)

C21:4 Describe what is taking place in sources E and G. Describe the strengths and weaknesses of these two different interpretations of the death of Richard III. Before answering this question it will help if you read about Polodore Vergil on page 68. (AT2 L7)

C21:5 Sources C, F and H tend to give a good impression of Richard III. However, historians who supported Henry Tudor might have wanted to give a bad impression of Richard III at the Battle of Bosworth. Describe some of the bad things they might have said about him. (AT3 L7)

Glossary

ABBEY Community of monks governed by an abbot, or of nuns under an abbess. Abbeys sometimes had schools and hospitals attached to them.

ARCHDEACON A clergyman who is the bishop's main assistant.

BALIFF The person in charge of the lord's demesne.

BARONS After the Norman Conquest, the tenants-in-chief were known collectively as barons.

BARREL VAULT A continuous arch that forms the roof of a building.

BAYEUX TAPESTRY A 230 feet (70m) long by 20 inches (0.5m) wide strip of linen that contains a series of embroidered pictures illustrating the Norman invasion of England. The tapestry includes pictures of 626 people, 190 horses, 37 ships and 33 buildings. It is believed that Bishop Odo, William the Conqueror's half-brother, organised the making of the tapestry. The embroidery was probably produced by a group of women from Canterbury in Kent in about 1090. After the tapestry was finished, it was taken to Bishop Odo's cathedral in Bayeux, France.

BENEDICTINES Monks who supported the ideas of St Benedict of Nursia. Formed in the 6th century, the Benedictine order emphasised obedience, communal worship and hard work.

BOON WORK Labour service provided by peasants to their lord at harvest time.

CANONISATION The pope had the power to declare that certain Christians were saints. The first canonisation took place in 993. Two famous saints, Thomas Becket and Francis of Assisi, were canonised within two years of their deaths.

CHARTERS Legal documents issued by a ruler or government. Charters mainly dealt with the ownership of land and the granting of privileges to towns.

CHIROGRAPH A recorded agreement between two parties. These agreements might concern the buying of property, arranging a marriage or the repayment of a loan. The document was written in duplicate and then both copies were cut in half (a wavy rather than a straight line). Attempted forgeries could then be checked in court by placing the two halves together.

CISTERCIANS Religious order founded in Citeaux in 1098. Cistercians were very hard-working and became successful farmers. Their monasteries tended to be built in remote areas.

CLERK A person who had been trained by the church but did not live in a monastery or work as a priest. Clerks were usually employed by lords of the manor to keep their accounts.

COURT ROLLS Documents that recorded details of court cases.

DEMESNE Land kept by the lord of the manor for his own use.

DOMESDAY SURVEY A detailed survey of the people of England and the property they owned. The survey was carried out in 1085-86 and was published in two volumes. One book is known as Little Domesday and contains the records of Norfolk, Suffolk and Essex. The second volume is known as Great Domesday and includes information about the rest of the country.

DOMINICANS An order of friars formed by St Dominic in 1217. Dominicans took a vow of extreme poverty and believed in converting people by using rational arguments. Dominican friaries were usually built in towns.

EXCOMMUNICATION Expulsion from the Christian Church. It was believed that all people who had contact with those who had been excommunicated would also suffer. Excommunicated people were therefore often treated like lepers.

FIEF Land held on condition of homage and the performance of services to a lord who continues to own the land.

FLAGELLANTS Groups of Christians who wandered from town to town, hitting themselves with leather thongs as punishment for their sins. The movement grew rapidly during the Black Death but was eventually successfully suppressed by the church.

FRANCISCANS Order of friars founded by St Francis of Assisi in 1209. Franciscans took a vow of extreme poverty. There was also an order of Franciscan nuns called Poor Clares.

GOTHIC Style of architecture in Europe that was very popular between the 12th and 16th centuries. The pointed arch, ribbed vaults and flying buttresses were important features of the Gothic style.

GUILD Organisation of workers who joined together in order to maintain standards of work and to support the interests of its members.

HERALDRY System developed during the Middle Ages that enabled individuals to be identified by symbols on shields and flags.

HERESY Religious beliefs that were in opposition to those held by the leaders of the Christian church. If heretics could not be persuaded to accept the traditional views of the Church they were likely to be executed.

HERIOT Payment by villein's family to the lord of the manor when the head of the family died. The payment of heriot, usually the family's best animal, enabled the family to continue using the lord's land.

HIGH TREASON A crime that involved any attempt to kill or remove a king from power.

HOMAGE The ceremony or oath by which a person agrees to become the lord's vassal.

INDULGENCE A paper issued by the Roman Catholic church that forgave people for sins they had committed. The selling of indulgences enabled the Church to raise a great deal of money during the Middle Ages.

INTERDICT Order issued by the pope. A country under interdict could not hold church services.

LOLLARDS A movement of Christians inspired by the teachings of John Wycliffe. Lollards believed that clergy should be allowed to marry, and criticised the wealth held by the church. Some Lollards also argued for pacifism and the redistribution of wealth.

MAGNA CARTA Charter issued by King John in 1215 that granted certain personal and political freedoms to the people under his rule.

MANUSCRIPT PAINTINGS Books in the early Middle Ages usually included painted pictures. However, by the end of the 15th century most books were printed rather than written by hand. Artists were no longer able to produce pictures at the speed required, and paintings in books were gradually replaced by engravings or woodcuts.

MARKET A place where goods were sold. A market was usually held once a week. The right to hold a market was granted by the king or a powerful lord. By the 14th century there were over 3,000 markets held every week in England.

MINSTREL A medieval musician. A minstrel was either attached to a lord's court or obtained money by visiting towns and villages.

MIRACLE PLAYS Stories from the Bible that were turned into plays. Miracle plays were usually performed in the market place by members of the town's guilds.

MOVABLE PROPERTY TAX A tax based on the value of people's property (excluding armour, jewels and robes) that could be moved. The rate of tax varied from as low as a twentieth to as high as an eighth of the value.

OUTLAW If a person failed to turn up at shire court to face charges brought against him, he or she would be declared an outlaw. The outlaw's property would be confiscated and given to the king. An outlaw lost all legal rights and anyone could kill him or her without punishment.

PAPAL BULL A letter from the pope that contains an important pronouncement.

PARISH An area under the the jurisdiction of a priest. By 1200 there were over 9,000 parishes in England.

PARDONER Travelling priest who sold letters from the pope forgiving people for their sins.

PIPE ROLLS The annual audit of the accounts of sheriffs and others who owed the crown money.

POLL TAX A tax levied on every person over a certain age.

PRELATE A high official of the church such as a bishop or abbot.

REEVE Official elected by the villeins. The reeve worked under the bailiff and was responsible for work carried out on the lord's demesne.

RELIC An object that was claimed by the church to be connected in some way to Jesus Christ or of one of the saints. People in the Middle Ages believed that these relics could work miracles.

RELIEF A sum of money paid to a dead man's lord in exchange for the right to inherit land and titles.

ROMANESQUE Style of architecture popular in Europe during the 11th century. The round arch and barrel vault were important features of the Romanesque style.

SERFS Unfree peasants who had to provide a whole range of services in exchange for the land that they used (for details see entry for *villein*). Serfs had originally been sold as slaves and had a lower status than villeins. In some areas serfs were described as slaves.

SCUTAGE A cash payment made to the king. Knights paid scutage instead of providing military service. This money was then used to hire professional soldiers.

SHERIFF The king's representative in a shire or county.

SIMONY Buying an official position in the church.

STEWARD The lord of the manor's senior representative. The steward was in charge of the manor court when the lord was absent.

TALLAGE An annual tax paid by villeins to the lord of the manor.

TENANT-in-CHIEF Somebody who held land directly from the king.

TESTIMONIALS Statements about people made by their lord or employer. People who travelled the country during the medieval period were treated with suspicion and were often arrested. If you had a good testimonial you would probably be allowed to continue your travels.

TITHES A tax of one-tenth of farm production. Tithes were paid to the local church.

TOLL Payment to the lord in order to gain permission to sell livestock.

VAULT An arched structure covering an interior space.

VILLEINS Unfree peasants who had to provide a whole range of services in exchange for the land that they used. This involved working on the lord's demesne without pay for several days a week. The villein also had to pay his lord many different taxes and fines: tallage; merchet; leyrewite; heriot etc. Villeins could not plead against their lord in court or leave the village without his permission.

WOODCUTS Woodcuts were made by drawing a picture on a block of wood. Parts of the block were cut away, leaving only the outline drawing. There were four main stages in the printing process: (a) the wood block was placed inside a press; (b) ink was rolled or dabbed onto the surface of the wood block; (c) a sheet of paper was placed on top of the wood block; (d) the press was closed and the weight on top of the block created a picture on the paper. Woodcuts first began to appear in Europe during the 15th century. By the 1480s most printed books contained woodcut pictures.

WRITS Letters that issued written commands. Most of these writs were issued by the reigning monarch. Henry II introduced the system where people had to sign and return these writs. They were then placed in the royal archives and could be consulted if any disputes arose.

Medieval Writers

Anglo Saxon Chronicles The chronicles are a collection of seven manuscripts written by monks living in England between the 9th and 12th centuries. The chronicles, written in the form of a diary, tell the story of England, and cover a period of over a thousand years. In some cases the entries were made several years after the events took place. Some passages of the various manuscripts are identical suggesting that a certain amount of copying took place. There are three manuscripts that cover the period of the Norman Conquest. It is believed that Version C was written in Abingdon near Oxford, Version D in Worcester and York, and Version E in Canterbury.

Geoffrey Chaucer was born in London in about 1340. After working for Elizabeth de Burgh (Edward III's daughter-in-law), Chaucer served as a soldier in France. Later he was employed by the king as a diplomat. This work involved Chaucer travelling all over Europe. After a period of translating poems written by famous foreign writers such as Boccaccio, Chaucer decided to write his own. In 1386 he began to write his most important work, *The Canterbury Tales*. The book is a collection of stories told by a party of pilgrims on a journey from Southwark to Thomas Becket's shrine at Canterbury. As Chaucer chooses characters from a whole range of different backgrounds, the book provides an important insight into the social, religious and economic conditions of the 14th century. Chaucer died in 1400.

Marie de France was born in France but spent nearly all her life in England (she was rumoured to be Henry II's illegitimate half-sister). Marie de France's 12th century romantic adventures were so popular that they were translated into several different languages. Copies of her books have been found written in French, English, Old Norse, German, Italian and Latin. Marie de France died in about 1190.

Jean Froissart was born at Valenciennes in France in 1337. At the age of twenty he was commissioned to write a book on warfare. Froissart came to England in 1360 where he entered the service of Philippa of Hainault, the wife of King Edward III. After eight years in England, Froissart travelled to France and Italy and eventually settled in the Netherlands. It was while he was in retirement in the Netherlands that he wrote his most famous work. Written in four volumes, Froissart's *Chronicles* deals with the history of Europe between 1326 and 1400. Most of the information in the book was based on interviews with people who had witnessed or had taken part in important events. In 1395 Froissart returned to England for the first time since 1369. The purpose of his visit was to present a copy of his work to Richard II. Froissart died in 1410.

Margery Kempe was born in Norfolk in about 1373. Married with fourteen children, Margery became a wandering preacher. She travelled all over Europe and eventually arrived in the Holy Land. Later, Margery, who was illiterate, dictated her life story to a scribe. The result was *The Book of Margery Kempe*, the first autobiography to appear in the English language. Margery died in about 1438.

Henry Knighton was the canon of St Mary's Abbey, Leicester. His chronicles start in the 10th century and end in 1395. Knighton was very interested in economic history, and his chronicles provide detailed information on prices, wages and taxation. He was extremely hostile to the Lollards and those involved in the Peasants' Revolt. Knighton died in 1396.

William Langland was probably born in Ledbury, Herefordshire in about 1332. Langland moved to London where made his living by singing songs at rich men's funerals. He also wrote poetry and is believed to be the author of *Piers the Plowman*. Written in West Midland dialect, the poem tells the story of Piers, a simple countryman. Langland was himself very poor and the poem provides a first-hand account of what life was like for ordinary people living in England during the 14th century. The poem also attacked the corruption of the nobility and leading members of the church. Langland died in about 1400.

William of Malmesbury was born in Wiltshire in about 1075. His father was a Norman and his mother came from England. William became a Benedictine monk at Malmesbury Abbey, and while working in its library he became interested in history. His books include *Deeds of the Kings of England* (449 to 1127) and *Recent History* (1128 to 1142). William was a conscientious historian. He searched for new primary sources including those produced in other countries. William's willingness to look critically at primary sources and his interest in cause and effect, helped him become one of the most important historians of the medieval period. William died in 1143.

William of Newburgh was born in Bridlington, Yorkshire in 1135. As a young man he joined the Augustinian priory at Newburgh. His book, *History of English Affairs* covers the period 1066 to 1197. William, unlike most historians of the time, tried very hard to write unbiased history. However, as he never left Newburgh priory he had to rely on what visitors told him. William of Newburgh died in about 1208.

Matthew Paris was born in about 1200. In 1236 Matthew became the chronicler of the abbey of St Albans. St Albans abbey was situated on the main road north from London. Many travellers stopped for the night at St Albans and Matthew Paris was able to collect a lot of information from them about what was going on in the rest of the country. Matthew's reputation as a historian grew and important people visited him, no doubt hoping that he would say nice things about them in his books. Those who visited him included King Henry III. However, Matthew disagreed with Henry's policy of appointing foreign advisers and he was often very critical of the king. As well as being a good writer, Matthew was a talented artist, and in the margins of his books he illustrated the text with drawings and paintings. Although he has been criticised for relying too much on rumour and gossip and being prejudiced against foreigners and friars, Matthew Paris is considered to be one of the most important historians of the medieval period. Matthew died in 1259.

Margaret Paston was the daughter of a wealthy family from Mautby in Norfolk. When her father died Margaret inherited his land. In about 1440 she married John Paston, who was also a large landowner in Norfolk. John Paston was a lawyer and spent a lot of time away on business, so Margaret had the responsibility of looking after the family estates. When they were separated Margaret kept in contact with John by letter. Over a hundred of these letters have survived and their contents provide an interesting insight into life in the 15th century. Margaret died in 1484.

Christine de Pisan was born in Venice, Italy in about 1365. She moved to Paris as a child of three when her father was appointed as King Charles V's doctor. Christine de Pisan's *The City of Ladies*, was the first history book written about women from the point of view of a woman. In the book Christine argues that male historians had given a distorted picture of the role played by women in history. The book attempted to redress the balance by providing a positive view of women's achievements. Christine's next book, *Three Virtues*, gave advice on how women could improve their situation. Christine wrote several other books including a book on military law and a biography of King Charles V. Her final work was a poem celebrating the achievements of Joan of Arc. Christine de Pisan died in about 1430.

William of Poitiers was born in Normandy in about 1030. After studying in Poitiers he became a Norman soldier. Later he became a priest and was eventually appointed as the archdeacon of Lisieux. When William became king of England in 1066 he invited William of Poitiers to become his personal chaplain. William of Poitiers' book *The Deeds of William, Duke of the Normans*, was published in about 1071. Although William of Poitiers was in Lisieux during 1066, his book provides the most detailed description that we have of the Battle of Hastings.

Ordericus Vitalis was the son of a Norman priest. Born in about 1075 he spent his early life in a Normandy abbey but eventually came to England and built his own monastery at Shrewsbury. Later he returned to Normandy where he spent the rest of his life. Between 1123 and 1141 he wrote *The Ecclesiastical History* which mainly dealt with the rule of William the Conqueror. Vitalis died in about 1143.

Polodore Vergil was born in Urbino, Italy in 1470. As a young man Vergil was employed by Pope Alexander VI. While working for the pope, Vergil developed a reputation as a talented writer. In 1502 Vergil was sent to look after the pope's affairs in England. Henry VII had been impressed with Vergil's books and paid him to write a history of England. The book, which was very carefully researched, took twenty-eight years to write. Most of the book is based on written sources that have not survived to the present day. Wherever possible, Vergil interviewed people who had taken part in important events and is a valuable source of information for the reigns of Edward IV, Richard III and Henry VI. Vergil died in Italy in 1555.

Thomas Walsingham was a Benedictine monk at St Albans Abbey. He continued the work started by Matthew Paris, the *Chronica Majora* (Greater Chronicle). His chronicles cover the period 1259 to 1422. He also wrote a history of the world from the creation to 1392. A conservative historian, Walsingham was extremely critical of the teachings of John Wycliffe and John Ball. Thomas Walsingham died in 1422.

Gerald of Wales was born in about 1147 at Marnobier Castle, Pembrokeshire. His father was a Norman knight, and his mother a Welsh princess. After his studies he became a teacher in Paris. Later he was appointed Court Chaplain to King Henry II. In 1185 Henry II ordered Gerald to accompany Prince John to Ireland. He wrote about these experiences in his books *The Topography of Ireland* and *The Conquest of Ireland*. Gerald was particularly interested in the military tactics used by both sides. Although Gerald was critical of the Irish his book shows concern for the way they were treated by John's army. Gerald also showed considerable sympathy for the Welsh in his book *Description of Wales*. In 1198 Gerald was elected as bishop of St. David's in Wales. However, Richard the Lionheart's officials, aware of Gerald's pro-Welsh opinions, did not allow him to take up the post. Gerald was offered several senior church posts in England but he refused and spent the rest of his life writing books. He died in about 1223.